THE BOOK OF
CREATIVITY

THE BOOK OF CREATIVITY

MASTERING YOUR CREATIVE POWER

BY
RASSOULI

THE BOOK OF CREATIVITY

Copyright © 2016 Rassouli
www.rassouli.com

All rights reserved.
Other than for personal use, no part of this book may be reproduced
in any way, in whole or part without the written consent
of the copyright holder or publisher.

Published by Blue Angel Publishing®
80 Glen Tower Drive, Glen Waverley
Victoria, Australia 3150
Email: info@blueangelonline.com
Website: www.blueangelonline.com

Edited by Leela Williams

Blue Angel is a registered trademark of Blue Angel Gallery Pty. Ltd.

ISBN: 978-1-922161-66-6

Borrow your beloved's eyes.
Look through them
and see the beloved everywhere.
You will feel no weariness,
no indifference,
for what was not appealing before
will begin to appear
in a new light.

RUMI

CONTENTS

Preface	9
Introduction	11
Life's Purpose	14
Creative Process	20
Power of Observation	26
Power of Imagination	31
Power of Visualization	36
Power of Intuition	45
Power of Inspiration	50
Power of Muse	57
Power of Discovery	64
Power of Desire	69
Power of Faith	74
Power of Sex	80
Power of Love	87
Power of Heart	93
Power of Uniqueness	99
Power of Freedom	106
Power of Limits	113
Power of Non-attachment	119
Power of Chaos	125
Power of Mind	131
Power of Block-busting	138
Power of Ego	144
Power of Surrender	152
Power of Silence	160
Power of Creativity	167
About the Author	175
Also available	177

PREFACE

I HAVE TEMPORARILY SET BRUSHES and paints aside to reflect on the experiences and ideas I feel would most inspire you to master your creative power. When you tap into the source of your immeasurable creativity it will bring more joy and satisfaction to your everyday life. I have no intention of formulating step-by-step guidelines, because I believe creativity is stimulated through inspiration rather than instruction.

I am not writing exclusively for those wanting to create grand works of art. Creativity can enhance every aspect of your life from moment to moment and thus, this book is for everyone. I am fortunate to have had a variety of experiences through which my artistic endeavors have evolved and they continue to open me to an inner vision that stimulates my own creative expression.

During my college days, I was taught the basic approach to writing an essay or a book. Once you have an idea of what you want to express, I was instructed to create an outline that set out the direction of the work before ever beginning to write. I no longer hold to such formalities, especially since my work is about mastering creativity. When I am painting, I simply surrender to my inner muse and follow as freely and truthfully as I am capable of doing. I am not influenced by a preconceived notion of what will come through. I play in a state of child-like innocence while applying strokes of color and form on the canvas. This book has evolved very much in the same manner.

Several years ago, while I was conducting a series of seminars on creative living at the University of Transformational Studies and Leadership in Southern California, I repeatedly heard from students who never thought they could be creative. They would tell me how their life and art became much more satisfying as they applied the creative approaches I recommended to them. Some stayed with me to help form the movement of Fusionart, which is about promoting and supporting a process that encourages individuals to utilize their creative power in all aspects of their lives. Within the past decade or so, the Fusionart concept has helped to stimulate the emergence of many blissful creative people across the globe.

I believe humanity will ultimately be united through the open sharing of one heart to another. How else are we to develop a deeper respect and appreciation of the differences in our traditions, our cultures, and our belief systems? How else shall we discover the true nature and the profound beauty that dwells within each one of us? The creative process can recognize and develop that beauty by clearing away whatever blocks it and by giving us the freedom to explore the depth and power of our feelings. Creativity can help us find a path of possibilities and give expression to what we see as beauty in a way that is natural to each of us.

My life began in the East, and my longings to create prompted me to cross an ocean in pursuit of my dream, to the western shores of California. I have since realized that our greatest achievements are truly possible when we are free to follow the guidance of our muse, which is the compassionate current of energy that unleashes our creative power and has the potential to unite us all. This book is intended as a guide, to help open the pathways toward that potential.

I invite you to wander with me, on a journey of spontaneity and mystery. Remain available to limitless creative possibilities along the way and life will unfold in remarkable ways. This process is similar to inviting the child within us to come out and play. We prepare for this by providing an inner atmosphere of freedom in which we may receive and express new perceptions and ideas, free of any sense of 'doing it right.' It is the playground where we can creatively manifest our dreams.

I am truly indebted to my long distance friend, Naomi Stone, whom I have never met in person, but who has lovingly supported me through writing and putting this book together. My hope is to inspire you to pursue your own deep and sometimes hidden desire to live creatively.

To create is like driving on a road that is not straight.
A creative person is one who enjoys going through every winding curve.

INTRODUCTION

To create is to reveal what we possess within!

ATTAR

SO MANY VARIABLES IN LIFE influence who we are and who we will eventually become. As we choose a direction or a path to follow, it helps to be conscious of what is most significant to us. We enter into a process of prioritizing our values by reflecting on the course of our upbringing, education and belief system. We examine our roots in light of the effect it has had on us and we remember what has touched us in deeper ways. Everything that happens to us comes into play in determining our path in life. Only the outer journey is visible to others.

The journey of creativity begins by turning inward and allowing the power that we hold within to guide us. We see through the outer veil into the mystery of a source far beyond what we can name. It is a life changing moment when we open to our inner creative power. What beckons us to express what we possess within? What is it that lures us to create? What calls the hidden beauty to be expressed in pouring through all creation?

Like a gardener longs to witness the flowering of the seed he has planted, we each long to glimpse the blossoming growth of the seed that has been placed within us. When we feel the creative seed stir, it excites us. Once we become aware of the power that has formed the universe, we align and identify with the energy of creation itself, and when we do that, we tap into the deeper source of our own lives. When we feel the flowing touch of creation, we come alive and glimpse a deeper vision. Through this experience, we encounter the power that inspires us to dream and to create. Energy generates sparks, and love becomes a catalyst to fan the flames into a fire that manifests the dream.

The spirit's journey toward expression is indeed a love story, because love is what truly awakens creativity. Rather than falling in love with an idol or becoming infatuated with something attractive, creative power falls into a flow of love that activates and touches everything. When that happens, we become a part of bringing the flow of love into an expressive form. I feel this in my heart every time I dip my brush into paint and allow creative energy to move through me, guiding what appears on the canvas. There is something mysterious and exhilarating within me that wants to be known. For me, it is the desire to encounter the beloved as it appears on my canvas.

As an artist, I am committed to reflecting on the messages that come through my heart, rather than relying merely on my technical ability as a painter. I was drawn to write about the process of surrendering to the creative spirit after working with many people through speaking engagements, classes, retreats, seminars, and personal encounters. I realized my story and process have had a positive impact on those interested in mastering their creative power, so I have taken on this new venture. I am now open to the creative energy guiding me as I write.

The beauty of the journey of spirit lies in the way it keeps expanding and enriching lives. Age is irrelevant to this awakening. The spirit of love moves us beyond time and space to set us free in a beautiful wilderness of creativity where we can engage in the dance of life.

The arts offer us creative opportunities to find the metaphors and the mediums of our self-expression. We are able to manifest and share the beauty of the spirit of love that dwells within us. Thus, the outer form becomes a kind of skin for our deeper surrender to the inner, living reality. When the creative process finds its clarity and is purified by our intentions, we are freed from our more personal ideas and wants, and we can focus on what is concealed inside. As artists, we bring it to the surface and give it life.

I consider creativity to be the wellspring of human power, for this is a truth I have experienced in my own life and in the expression of my art. When we allow the inner self to become the generator of our artistic expressions, a power develops within us that moves and guides us in every challenge we encounter. This happens through a flow of creative elements, through an empowering energy, through the very breath and life force of the universe. I believe creativity is the river to freedom that we all must cross to develop self-satisfaction. When we wade and surrender into the flow of that river through the currents of love, we allow it to create and bring meaning to everything around and within us.

Those who choose to use the thinking mind as the ultimate source of power – as stimulating as it can be – face losing something wonderful, mysterious and transformational that moves us beyond our mental understanding alone, and is the ultimate energy that creates the universe. When we blunder into the power of divine intellect, we are on holy ground. According to scripture, the angel Lucifer was thrown out of Heaven for trying to steal the power to compete with God. In wanting to be God, Lucifer was misusing and betraying the intimacy of love he had been given. He glimpsed the infinite power and he longed to keep the secret for himself in order to control others. When we only use the thinking mind, we risk losing everything. The highest and ultimate love is the comfort, the companion, the security, and the energy of the source of all creation. Pure love is inclusive and comes as a gift of grace. We surrender into this flow to share in the generosity of the creative power, for it is not in our human ability to create a universe.

No matter what method we use, whether it is seduction, domination, oppression or cruelty, to force another to submit, we steal the gift and grace of the creative power, and deprive them of this incredible inner presence by making them dependent upon someone else in order to live. To become a messenger who reflects and reveals the creative power that is hidden within all of us is truly a mission worth sharing.

We are formed by our relationship with ourselves, and it is only through opening our hearts to each other that we can share and express the beauty that we are. Creation has left us an endless stream of clues to help guide us in finding the rhythm to be free and to create. Each of us will discover the creative path in our own unique ways. Together, we form a community of 'Fusionartists' who support each other with the love that empowers the journey. We are all invited to become artists infused with the amazing gift and energy of this creativity.

LIFE'S PURPOSE

The greatest danger for most of us is not that our aim is too high and we miss it, but that it is too low and we reach it.

MICHELANGELO

WHO AM I? WHY AM I in this world? What is the reason for this life? What distinguishes me as human from animals? These are some of the questions we ask ourselves at times. Without convincing answers, many give up thinking about them and continue to live the way they are expected to, paying little or no attention to finding the purpose of their life. To certain people, these questions become so vital that they spend most of their lives in search of the answers. Eventually, the search will lead them within where they can tap into the source of creativity in themselves.

In my early teens, I would take a trail that led to the top of a mountain near my home and there I would sit in silence on a rock where I had a panoramic view of the entire city below me. Here, I would spend hours questing for answers, daydreaming and often entering into a kind of trance state thinking about what was ahead for me and what kind of life I might have.

As time passed, those questions would rise again and again, but I never could come up with satisfying answers. I could not find the context or the perspective in which to really discover the truth I was seeking. This continued until I finally began to realize that I was living out the answers of my questions, and one of them was the underlying purpose of my existence.

Every time I experience moving toward the unknown, something within me comes alive. It is like the bewildering influence of love, which can send me spinning into a new existence. I may set out to find the mental answers to the question of why I am here, but I feel much more alive when I am on some kind of a quest guided by the longings deep within me. They lure me on and draw me into the excitement of the unknown. When this happens, everything around me suddenly becomes more exciting and appears to have more meaning. I am on alert, keeping a vigil to watch for clues and to recognize the signs that will help to discern my next move, eager to discover what is around the next bend in the road.

As I write, I wonder whether the purpose of my existence is to follow the mystery that awakens my heart, my senses and my soul to the discovery of who I truly am, who I am becoming and who I could be. It isn't something static that is awaiting my arrival. It is something unseen, like the wind moving the leaves, which is changing me and urging me forward. I feel that my purpose is to be fully and completely alive to the changing face of creation and the energy that moves it. Even more than the call of something new, I am compelled by the powerful invitation to feel the love that moves the energy of creation and is transformed by it.

As a part of the network of life on this planet, we are constantly experiencing an expanding awareness of our surroundings – as it all happens! Perhaps there is no ultimate or final goal. Perhaps we are learning to adapt to this adventure that changes as we live it. Over and over we have been told to value our experience of the moment as it is a sacred event in an evolving existence. That there may be no final goal was a revelation, more than I ever expected or anticipated when I first pondered why I was here.

The boy that I was has become an older man who continues to gaze, but from a new perspective, at an incredible and astounding universe. I no longer seek to imagine my lifeline from its beginning to its ending. I have no idea where or how it will end! This is the thrill of the unknown for me. Rather than frightening me, it excites me and makes me feel ageless!

Every human being is in search of some kind of happiness, joy or pleasure, even if we are unaware of it. Once we accept that we are a vital part of this earth and surrender into the creative experience that guides us, we will grow more and more capable of living the life of our dreams. This is the first indication that our purpose in this life is to live fully and compassionately as an inseparable part of the universe, while we continue to attend to our own role as an advocate for its evolution. Everyone's purpose is based on an individual instinct for survival and the deeper desire for a meaningful existence. Creative energy propels each of us towards our purpose. The aim is to be aware of it.

We are all connected with the creative source before we are born and the connection continues throughout our life time, even though we are often alienated from this truth. Those who remain awake, and are consciously aware of this, are among the most fortunate people to have ever embarked on the journey of living.

There is no doubt that we are all affected by our own setting, culture, traditions, beliefs, and by those who live around us. Ultimately, the direction we take is determined by our willingness to build on this to become a part of the collective and global experience of everyone and everything that exists. We can't hold on to the details or be aware of the subtle and unseen ways in which this happens, but we can have faith that the creative process will always allow us to be a part of this unfolding. Our dreams determine the level of our greatness, for they hold the essence of life as it is arising from the soul. As they say, *"You will be more disappointed by the things that you didn't do than by the ones you did."*

Once we decide that our life's purpose is more than making it through each day, we begin to expand beyond our small personal goals to allow space for a greater plan to unfold. We can rarely grasp that plan, and there is no need to. Once the energies of creation are given free range, life moves into a realm that is not subject to scale, for it is beyond measurement. In this realm, life progresses as a spiral of expansion and contraction, blooming and blossoming and changing colors, mixing and matching and creating new species.

Life can feel empty to those who don't grasp a higher purpose in life. These are the people who are looking for something, but don't really know what it is. They feel no real joy in life and even something as simple as getting out of the bed in the morning and facing a new day can feel like a burden. They are confused and disoriented, because they have no direction. They desperately need to find meaning in their life, yet one can't simply make up or pretend to have a purpose just because they are told they should have one.

Purpose gives a person the strength to carry on through difficult conditions, as well as through the unexpected changes we face every day. To find purpose, one is required to tap into the source of creation. This energy has the creative power to move our lives in a way we cannot do alone.

Everyone looks to better themselves and to improve their lives. However, purpose is definitely not about only receiving worldly benefits. We are here on planet Earth to 'put out' or express in some creative way. The more we reach for success as some kind of self-promoting target or goal, the more we miss the fullness of the life we are given.

Success, like happiness, cannot be pursued. It only comes as the result of personal dedication to something greater than us, or as the result of surrendering to a higher power. If we want love from other people, we need to love them. If we want more joy in life, we need to give joy to others, and if we want to make money, we need to help others to have what they need.

In my younger days, I explored all kinds of possibilities, thinking it would help me to discover my purpose in life. While I was going to college, I worked as a draftsman in an architect's office. It paid the bills, but I hated the job. I wanted to be a great painter just like many of my contemporaries who were successfully living their dreams. I wanted what they had, a passion that was reflected on canvas, tremendous love for life and a solid connection to their art.

My struggle to find my purpose continued until I realized this was not something I could simply figure out in my head. It was a great breakthrough when I recognized the problem was not that I didn't know what to do to realize my purpose in life, it was the way I was going about trying to reach it.

Life's purpose is not something we can think our way to discovering. We align with it by taking steps in the direction of what we truly want, and removing the obstacles that are in the way. I did that when I gave up a successful architectural practice to follow my heart's desire. I was finally able to move toward my life purpose when I took the steps fearlessly, one after another to explore my dream. I can now gracefully admit that the way is not found by simply looking for it, but by doing it, by living what we love to do.

One of the main causes of procrastination is overthinking. Should I try this? Would this work? What if it turns out to be a failure? What if it does not bring any income? Success in life comes to those who fearlessly try new things without being attached to the end result. Clarity comes through exploration. Results are revealed only after the action is taken. Dwelling on what to do only pushes us further away from reaching our ultimate purpose in life. I stopped watching television and began painting, sculpting, designing and writing every night until I collapsed from fatigue. By doing and trying everything, I learned that my true passion was indeed painting. I had to stop wondering and take action, before I could realize that painting was my joy.

While talking or writing about creating helps us find our reason for being, taking action gives us purpose and brings a deeper meaning to our existence. Action takes us to new heights and moves us beyond the rational mind. Action is a climax of intention that exalts and lifts us beyond what we could ever imagine. It is not possible to envision what may be shared and expressed through creative living. Action brings growing excitement, a feeling of lightness and a spreading of invisible spirit wings that we feel as joy. In creativity, we find ourselves laughing without knowing why. We smile the enchanting smile of one who has a secret and our eyes shine with the light of love because we are, at last, living our purpose. We feel a blessed assurance in our hearts.

Sometimes, at the height of success, people still feel that something is missing in their life. This can be because they are trying to stay with the one thing they think they are meant to be doing. This idea can easily become a block on the way to reaching our full potential. I don't consider myself only as a painter. I actually create in multimedia and paint, sculpt, design, write, coach and conduct seminars. All of these activities bring me joy and help me express my passion for creating. I believe that passionate living and doing what we truly enjoy doing is the path to finding purpose. By jumping in and giving things a try, we eliminate repetitive thinking. The 'what ifs' and 'maybes' will no longer be at the center of our thoughts. Instead, our minds and hearts will revolve around loving life in its fullness. This prevents the resistance of the unknown and encourages a more intimate involvement with what is happening in the moment. This is the way to overcome the feeling that we are missing something in life.

The best source for discovering our true purpose is the whisperings of our hearts. Through communion with the heart, we can seek within to discover what it is we truly love to do. What is our deepest longing? Hopefully, we can take a step of faith to seek out our dreams and live them as fully as we are able. Inspiration comes to a glad heart and a peaceful soul. We experience more joy and are more inspired when we follow the guidance of the heart.

We are called to find the energy to live our dream with purpose and meaning. We can then explore creative ways of expressing who we are for the pure joy of sharing, whether it is through music, art, heartfelt service to others, through designing buildings, gourmet cooking, sculpture, dance, humor, writing, or any one of the endless opportunities available to us in this life.

When we grow closer to realizing our purpose, we naturally move into a higher zone of creativity. When we are able to imagine doing what we truly enjoy, we develop that part of our character that actually brings us joy. Every morning, as I take my daily walk, I formulate in my mind certain things that I feel passionate about doing that day. Even if I don't do all of them, they still develop positive feelings within me by reminding me of what I love to do and that I have given myself permission to do them.

Learning about the lives of those we admire is another approach I consider valuable for finding one's purpose and reason for being is. This is an important way to discover what we appreciate in others as well as in ourselves. We are attracted to certain qualities because we feel they may help us to develop our own path. When we follow in the footsteps of our personal idols and heroes, the journey of creativity becomes much more exciting than simply trying to find the way by ourselves.

As a child, Rembrandt became my idol, especially after I read that he once used his own blood to paint the fiery color in the light of the sunset, because his father took his red paint away from him. It was a great inspiration for me to learn about young Rembrandt's resourcefulness and the act of drawing on his own creative energy to express what he saw in the intensity of color radiating from the sun.

Sometimes people point us in a certain direction by the ways they identify and describe us. When people comment that we have an eye for detail, or that we have a great sense of humor, or that we have the ability to listen creatively, we are able to consciously access abilities and qualities that we may not have been aware of before. In this way, we are encouraged in new directions.

Paying attention and being present to these kinds of comments and actions, allows us to bridge the distance between our human life and the divine creative source from which we flow. Thus, a stray remark can help us surrender to the beauty of the unknown and to trust the secrets of the creative process. Some discover it is within their nature to be a mother and delight at giving birth to a new life. Another person, like Mother Teresa, may discover it is within their nature to help ease the pain of others in a life of service. This kind of revelation is where we begin to tap into the source to find the love and courage we need to master our creative power.

The journey to love is the process of becoming aware of this flowing energy. We learn to recognize the clues and feel the changes within ourselves when we allow love to guide us. We realize that obstacles are part of the journey, rather than a block to the flow of our creativity. Suddenly, we love the rock in the middle of the road, and we want to take action that will connect us with it. This is the glorious discovery of awakening the creative power of the heart!

When our life's purpose is known to us, we rejoice in our potential for an exuberant life. Every morning, I jump out of bed in anticipation of going to my studio to create. I keep on creating until late at night when my legs carry my weary body from the studio to my house. I make the journey in the dark, and along the way, I sometimes lie down on the path to look at the trees, noticing the gentle sway and shimmer of the leaves. I look at the stars glowing with a light from a distance I cannot even imagine. An image begins to form in my mind's eye. I feel the stirring of something creative moving inside of me. The process of creating is not limited to painting; it is in the journey of imagination that launches me into unknown territory. Every discovery is an adventure. The next day, I want to relive the experience, and so I allow its expression in a new creative way.

We are here to create, so that the secrets of life might show themselves in a stream of revelation. No matter what medium we choose, we are drawn and attracted into the creative process. The moment guides us. When I look at a painting I have just finished, I bear witness to a creation that grew from a mysterious flow of energy moving through me. Words flower into images, and beauty guides us into the unknown. We are created to touch and be touched by this mystery. We are attracted to that which guides us to live and express our joy. We discover what inspires us. Inspiration literally means "to breathe in." Being inspired is a process of taking a part of life into ourselves and fleshing out its secrets through the act of creating. This affects how we perceive everything, and determines whether or not we will welcome the future.

Human beings find the rhythm of their expression in the way they allow the creative process to move them forward as energy manifests through them through some artistic medium. It is a subtle process of listening, observing and paying attention to the sensations that moves us to find the creative flow that defines our life and determines who we were created to be and who we will eventually become. When we feel empowered to live a creative life, it forms new connections that align us with the source of life itself. Instead of trying to rise above others, we strive to share the gift of vision and the joy that flows from it.

The creative process happens when the inner power is free to leap and move the way a child moves within the womb of a mother, stirring and touching what is forming within it. In reality, creative energy is far more subtle and not restrained by the limits of the womb. It is something in progress, evolving within, that is unseen and unknown, yet it is experienced as the presence of the power to create. When we are perfectly still and silent, it is glowing within us, abiding and dwelling as a hidden aspect of life itself. If we could isolate it, we might behold this glow, as the spark of a deeper fire seeking expression.

A creative life is a conversation with a presence that dwells within us and attunes our longings so that we recognize what is attracting us. We develop through a collective and universal flow that each one of us is bringing into being in our own unique way. Everything that happens in life – whether it affects us positively or negatively – is a catalyst that moves us to respond. When we live creatively, we seek ways to allow a response to manifest through us and be integrated into our lives within our human capacity to express it. We do not create for our own edification and glory. Rather, we creatively reflect and express to raise our own awareness and to have the opportunity and privilege of being able to share with others what gives our life meaning.

CREATIVE PROCESS

*Only when he no longer knows what he is
doing, does the painter create good things.*

EDGAR DEGAS

CREATIVE ENERGY FLOWS, SPONTANEOUSLY AND intuitively prompting the subconscious to transcend the restrictions of rules, ideas, methods, and beliefs to invite new and fresh possibilities into expression. Creativity partners with imagination and experience to bring originality and uniqueness into what we do and how we live. It is the passion and divine spark that invites us to create.

Creativity is a spiritual and psychological journey beyond mastering the technique of one art form or another. To create is to experience things in new ways and from a different perspective. Creativity is all about spontaneous expression.

Many people think of creativity as something artistic, lofty, intelligent, and unusual and beyond understanding, which only artists, writers, and performers are gifted with. In reality, creativity is a perception available to everyone, which helps us to see new solutions to problems and be innovative in our responses to life. It is said that we are created in the image of our creator, which implies that every one of us has the potential to create.

The function and basic instinct of every organism is to reproduce itself, and to create what is needed for survival. The very first thing we do, as soon as we are born, is to breathe – inhaling oxygen and exhaling carbon dioxide. That breath helps in the growth and development of plant life. Trees create oxygen, provide shade, and some bear flowers and fruit. As human beings, we are gifted with the ability to create, even though we may be unaware of this in the beginning. We have the potential to become a part of the process that has created the earth, which is a self-sustaining and living organism.

The question each one of us faces is how and what we can contribute to this process. The universe reflects the answer to this question wherever we look. We gaze at what has formed around us, and sense that we also need to reflect some expression of ourselves. We live and experience who we are as we grow and evolve, and we share that on physical, mental, emotional, and spiritual levels. We discover that our bodies, hearts, minds, souls, and spirits carry secrets and hidden messages about who we are.

The wellspring of creativity is a source that exists deep within everyone. The act of creation unleashes an energy that is capable of setting everything in motion. As artists, we learn to tap into this source. There is a fluctuating wave of expansions and contractions that is continually making and eliminating to achieve a balance on Earth. There is a cosmic rhythm constantly making room for something new to happen, to be born, to manifest, or to come into form. When we become sensitive to these cycles and align with that energy, we are able to share in this creative process.

We seek ways to remain open to the flow of this energy, and we surrender to its movement throughout the universe. When we trust this process and stay open to it, the creative energy does the work it was designed to do. That same potential exists within all life forms here on Earth. Sometimes we become afraid of what we don't understand, and we close down and block the power from working in ways that we don't even realize. Our perception varies according to where we live, what we believe, what our traditions are, and what our cultural values might be.

Those mystics who have lived and experienced the mystery of life, believe that we have been separated from the original source from which all life has developed. Some set out on a pilgrimage or quest to connect with the creator of all life and awaken their cellular memory of the beginning of creation. This source is a living energy that has been set in motion. What activated the first heart to start beating? Was there a time of nothingness before life began? We live in the mystery of these questions.

In order to realize our freedom to create, we each have obstacles to overcome. Some of us have been raised to be receptive to mystery and are comfortable with not truly knowing the answers to the deeper questions. Others immediately become drawn to owning and having and living as consumers. The channels of communication and perception can be clogged with too many thoughts and possessions, just like our arteries become clogged by foods too rich for our digestive systems. Some people are considered geniuses and child prodigies, and they can create through a clear channel in astounding ways. They are naturally open, because they don't know any other way to be. We could take a lesson from the way they adapt to the physical world from within.

I recall a story my grandmother would tell me to put me to sleep. It was the story of three princes whose father, the king, had told them that inside a certain well there was a ring, and whoever found it would be his heir to the crown. The first child, the oldest, was lowered into the well. Halfway down the well, he screamed to be pulled up, for a fire inside the well was burning him. So they pulled him up. The second son, who had witnessed the experience of his brother, told them not to pull him up until he shook the rope. As he was lowered into the well, he could feel the fire and tried to bear the heat. Finally, it became unbearable, he pulled on the rope and they quickly pulled him up.

The third son, who had seen what happened to the other two, instructed that if he shakes the rope, or screams to be pulled up, they should cut the rope and release him. He was lowered in the well and felt the fire like the other two brothers. As he grew closer to the unbearable heat of the fire, he screamed to be pulled out, which was the signal to cut the rope. As his connection with the outside world was severed, he fell straight through the fire in a moment and landed in a garden more magnificent than he could have imagined, even in a dream. At that point, he had no need or desire to return.

This story has always been a metaphor of creative power for me. As we take steps away from what we have taken as a standard in our life, we face new possibilities. In order to find the way, we need to face whatever opposes us. It is a painful process, for we have traditionally accepted that our identity is who we appear to be on the outside.

As an artist, my life is all about creating. I love to create, and I have no resistance to surrendering to the creative process that guides my expression. I paint, but I am not in the business of making paintings to sell. I paint because I love to engage with the medium in order to express what is flowing through my heart and soul. I am energized by what I do, and I have great fun doing it. I have a kind of relationship with the canvas, and my paints and brushes, and my hands and fingers become instruments expressing my love for beauty and causing my heart to overflow with joy!

Being creative is not learning to do something in a certain way that meets the expectations of others. It is about discovering a certain power inside of us that makes us unique. Creativity is about utilizing great variations within a process as a way to express who we are. There is a thrill in creating that leaves one energized and feeling exalted at being a part of such an amazing process. It employs our senses, engages our minds, opens our hearts, and gently awakens us.

The source of creativity is contained in mystery and cannot be explained. This secret is sheltered in the unknown aspects of who we are. We journey into the mystery to allow the creativity that has been infused and embedded within us to express our hidden longings. We allow it to take place in order to create within the ongoing process that changes us. It is our challenge to allow spirit to manifest within us and to let it move us beyond the fear of the unknown. We have no idea what anyone else's expression is meant to be, or wants to be, until it manifests and appears to coming through them.

Sometimes during my creativity sessions, I ask participants to paint on a canvas with their eyes closed. If they open their eyes to see the painting, they are not to go back to work on it any more. Painting with closed eyes means they cannot compare their artwork with what they had in mind. They follow their intuition, not their rationality to paint. As they are painting, they perceive a perfect image in their mind, but what they see with open eyes is different from what they pictured. This practice is very helpful in learning not to judge what they are creating while they are doing it.

The creative process allows for infinite creations to form and reify through the intensity of longing. Business-minded people create new and inventive ways to develop their enterprises. Doctors create new ways of discovering the possible causes of a patient's symptoms. Teachers create new ways of helping students to learn. Since life is an ongoing process of transformation, we do not discover everything at once, but continue uncovering different aspects of ourselves as we interact with existence and move along the way.

Creative power is like the sun, shining to reach for the heart of all that is expanding and ready to burst open, to sprout or blossom. The creative response to life is like the cloud that rains and softens the seed in order to produce and nurture plants, flowers, leaves, and all that grows upon the earth, including us. The process of creativity naturally seeks ways to develop a balance between the act of clearing the passage and finding a great variety of ways to manifest the energy that is flowing through us into something amazingly new. It softens our perception so that we see it compassionately. Small and vulnerable versions of life that need care, awaken our desire to love and nurture, be it a sprouting plant, a tiny kitten, or the miracle and innocence of a new baby.

Creating is a transformational expression that humanizes us. There is no final goal to reach, although there are many helpful points to consider and instincts to follow along the way. To live creatively, we need to discover the clues that will guide us and help us to express what is in our hearts, which is amazingly varied within each individual. The greatest joy that one experiences on the creative path has to do with the breakthroughs that appear suddenly and spontaneously!

The flow of creativity needs to remain free of contamination so that love can find free expression, in much the same way as water finds the most natural course, or light slips through the openings that are open to it. Love is certainly the most powerful agent of transformation for opening the flow within us and for inviting us to feel and respond to the creative desire. When love invites, we draw out the response, and when someone sees that excitement in us and shares in what we create, it stimulates us to become more than before. Joy breaks us open and expands us, and playfulness and a lightness of being surrounds us with an energy that frees us to create and to love without the obstacles of self-doubt and fear.

Creating is not only about expressing or manifesting something. It also includes the way in which we experience what happens to us and how we respond to it. When we bring something into focus, we use our imagination, we become inspired and we are empowered by our creative energy. If we do not implement or express the ideas, images or visions presented to us, but let them slip away or become blocked in some way, we may still be imaginative, but we cease to be creative.

People think that artists are more creative than others not because of their talent, but because of the skill and technique they use to manifest and express their creations. Yet, when the circumstances are right, combining technical ability and skill with creative energy can occur in almost any endeavor, by anyone, whether it is for business or pleasure. We need to find the freedom to be fully aware of this choice and possibility that awaits us!

Two major powers that make us create are love and the commitment to flow with it. The more joy we get from the process of developing creativity, the more innovative the result will become. Each time that we achieve better results, it invariably stimulates further ideas. In its wholeness, the creative process involves discovering ways to make it more fun while doing whatever we are doing at the time. Even if what we are doing is already fun, doing it in a new and different way can make it even more enjoyable.

My very first art teacher was an artist who painted miniature paintings. He taught me a certain way to see colors in patches without the limitation of forms. One of the techniques I learned from him was to stand with my feet wide apart, to bend over and to look through the opening between my legs to look at what was behind me. I was to paint what I saw from that position.

Through this exercise, I learned to look at things from a different perspective, from various new angles, and from all different directions. As my mind was not limited to discerning and seeing the patterns of nature in only one absolute way, I began to observe my environment as patches and areas of colors, rather than as forms or recognizable shapes. The process of painting became much more fun, for I was painting things upside down and not simply copying forms or shapes in a recognizable way. It was very amusing for me to see images created on paper that did not look at all like what I would see right side up. That process was particularly helpful in developing my imagination.

Creativity often involves breaking rules and moving beyond other people's beliefs and ideas as well as our own. It also challenges and confronts the expectations of others, because it moves us out of our comfort zones. We need to be open to possible disappointment in order not to betray the truth of what is trying to express itself through us. Risk incites growth. We are like plants that need to push through the darkness of the soil to feel the sun. If we adhere to already set standards and remain within the limitations imposed on us by others, we are not truly sharing in the creative process. We are conforming and being obedient to someone else's expectations and ideas of what is right for us. We try to please our captor instead of responding to the longing for life flowing through our hearts.

The most important thing about the creative process is the belief that we are undertaking a great work while doing it. If we don't think it is worthwhile, there is no way in the world that we would truly want to continue and finish it. What is interesting is that once our artwork is done, we may realize that it is not the greatest work in the world, but we accept it as just another one of our creations.

Creativity demands the freedom and the right to make mistakes, for it involves trying something new that is outside the boundary of normal standards and may never have been tried before. Our bumps and bruises and disappointments help to prepare and encourage us to reach beyond the safety zones.

To prepare for the journey of creativity, I usually spend time arranging and rearranging my paint jars, brushes and overall workspace until I have the urge to begin playing with color on the canvas. The secret to constantly creating is the willingness to change, and being able to change.

As we grow older, we become more nostalgic, which tends to make us focus more on the past and we are not as confident that we have a present life that is worth reflecting. Every time an image shows up on my canvas easily, I become suspicious because that usually means it reflects something I have already painted. When images are unsettling, and I am excited about what I'm doing, that means it's going to be an interesting artwork. When a new idea comes through, hope makes the heart swoon and the mind expand around it. Daydreaming helps tremendously to stimulate new possibilities as we work. Everyone is an artist, but there is a difference between artists who create and artists who only carry new ideas around in their thoughts.

I often bounce back and forth between the excitement of creating something new and the suspicion that perhaps my instincts are off and I am headed in the wrong direction. This continues until I suddenly feel more clarity in my imagination as if the sky has opened and I can hear the music of angels. Of course there are other times when a work is uninspired and remains unfinished.

Every time someone tells me they have writer's block, I suggest they just paint or write for the purpose of throwing it in the waste basket. I tell them not to be concerned if it does not look good to them, and not to be concerned about ruining it. Creating art takes the efforts of a fully developed discipline and strong faith. All art works begin to come to life when you are creating. If you get out of the way and don't try to control what happens, the energy will guide you in making the next move. American composer Aaron Copland said *he didn't finish compositions as much as he abandoned them*. He got out of the way to allow the music to guide the process.

As living organisms, we are deeply integrated and connected with creation itself. When we create, we explore both the known and the unknown possibilities of forming a spiritual connection between our own personal experience and our acquired knowledge. This experience orients us to the folding, and unfolding, and the unveiling of the beauty of an expanding life. It becomes like the rhythm of a dancing heartbeat or like the deepening colors of the rising and setting of the sun. The universe continues to reveal its mystery to us as we live and experience each day. The ocean expresses a rhythmic movement in the waves as they touch the shore and circle back into the ocean again. As we surrender, we become aligned with the energy of creation in a very intimate way, and we become aware of the flow of creative energy that seems to be painting the universe with the colors of love.

POWER OF OBSERVATION

The business of art is rather to understand Nature and to reveal her meanings to those unable to understand. It is to convey the soul of a tree rather than to produce a fruitful likeness of the tree. It is to reveal the conscience of the sea, not to portray so many foaming waves or so much blue water. The mission of art is to bring out the unfamiliar from the most familiar.

KHALIL GIBRAN

CREATIVE PROCESS BEGINS WITH EXPERIENCING the environment imaginatively. The ability to perceive the world in new ways is a special quality that develops artists, scientists and creative entrepreneurs. By experiencing our surroundings imaginatively, we are able to bring together what may seem like unrelated forms, ideas, and happenings to create new perceptions and solutions. Creative observation is about seeing things in a personal or uncommon manner, rather than the way others see. Creativity allows for the expansion of our collective vision. Observation is the outward thrust of daring to look and move beyond our closed circle of habitual comfort.

By developing our imagination we become attuned to trusting our intuition. This allows us to be present to the moment and to respond in a fresh way to every situation — very similar to the way nature evolves. As a result, we become inspired and enthusiastic about whatever we are doing, and we are able to bring a positive energy to it. As we experience joy, the fulfillment moves us to want to share the process with others. We find our own unique way of expressing it and that becomes our art.

Picasso used to sit by the sea, observe the sunrise, and then walk back to his studio, which was a short distance from the shore. While walking back, the first thing that caught his eyes and attracted him often became the inspiration for his next work of art. The creative power in Picasso was developed through his special way of observing everything around him as having the potential for another masterpiece.

Creativity relies heavily on the development of the imagination. Although we are all born to create, we need to nurture this particular attribute through the special way we observe our environmental conditions and the way we use certain techniques to reflect it in our work and in our interpersonal relationships. Artists allow their creativity to take root and flourish through their abilities and whatever is available to them. Creating something that is considered novel and innovative is the result of free play that stems from imaginative observation.

The first time I held a camera in my hand, I was six years old. The camera was a German-made view camera that I received as a birthday gift from my parents. I was so excited that in the first hour, I took pictures of whatever I could see around me. This included flowers in the garden, my family members, the chicken I had as a pet and everything else that I could see as a potential photograph.

My excitement, however, did not last long. After a few weeks of taking pictures that were more or less reflecting what was around me, I became bored with the limitation of the camera and the repetitious images of the photographs. Perhaps what was causing me to lose interest was my pre-conceived idea of how things should look in my pictures. I was only taking photographs of what I could see around me, instead of bringing imagination to the use of the camera.

One day, while I was playing with my pet chicken in the garden, I felt like taking a picture of myself with my pet. Since no one was around to take the picture and the camera had no automatic shutter, I came up with a way to take it myself. I tied the shutter knob to a string and placed the camera on a chair and sat a few feet away from it, holding the tip of the string in one hand and the chicken in the other hand. I then pulled the string to move the shutter to take the picture. I must have pulled the string too hard. It caused the camera to fall off the stand, but while it was falling, it had taken a photograph.

When the film was developed and I received the photos, one of them was a weird picture, which showed the tail of the chicken with my hand holding it, some plants and flowers on the side, and what looked like a long pipe, which was the close up of the string tied to the camera. That picture turned out to be the one that caught lots of attention. All the other photographs looked normal, while anyone who saw that particular photo, paid more attention to it and made a remark about it. The interest that my family and friends showed to that unusual photo encouraged me to begin taking pictures of isolated parts or portions of things rather than the whole subject. It opened me to the possibilities and fascination of the observation and variation implicit in a single vision.

Following that experience, I became excited about photography and began to seek out different ways of observing my environment through the process of picture taking. Sometimes I would take a picture while jumping up in the air, other times I would lie down on the floor and look through the camera as if I were seeing through the eyes of my chicken. From that time on, I was mostly looking for unusual images rather than the ones we normally observe.

After a while, this creative vision became very natural for me and without realizing it, I began capturing moments rather than subjects. I was pulling away from focusing on a point of interest and becoming more attracted to abstract shapes and forms. Those who viewed my photographs were finding their own points of interest in them, and I enjoyed hearing their impressions of what they were observing. This was a way that I could see through their eyes and they could see through mine.

Through that method of observation, I became attuned to seeing things in ways that made everything look more interesting to me. From then on, I was noticing certain beauty in unexpected objects, people or places. I was taking pictures of them and then gazing at the produced images for long periods of time. The process helped me to discover incredible patterns and forms in carpets and rugs, and find beauty in the cracks on the wall and even in the shapes of water stains on the floor.

It was because of that childhood experience that even today, when I am about to start a new painting, I stare at the surface of the blank canvas for a while. To enjoy the process even more, I usually have my canvases primed in black, rather than the usual white that most artists use. I continue staring, opening my vision, until I begin to discover images on the canvas. Sometimes I turn the canvas around and look at it from all different directions in search of the most attractive or interesting images. I have found this exercise quite effective for the development of my imagination. Of course, the forms that I see on the black canvas usually come alive and change into something else the moment I touch them with the first stroke of the paint brush. According to Thoreau, *"It's not what you look at that matters, it is what you see!"*

From early childhood, I somehow managed to see the world through creative eyes, which meant looking at things a little differently to the way my sister and parents were observing them. It sometimes meant seeing things in a bizarre way and being more confrontational with my classmates. I was seeing stars in different colors, while my sister was seeing all of them yellow. I was seeing the image of a horse galloping in the sky, while my playmates were only seeing clouds.

Noticing things in new ways leads to an interest in more detailed observations. Every time something new and unusual is perceived, it feels like a new discovery. Whatever appears before the eyes becomes attractive in a totally new way. An appreciation and a taste for certain types of images develops, and there comes a longing to see beauty in everything. Bringing conscious awareness to what we see and perceive creates an energy that has an effect on what is observed. It feels relational. Mystics use the phrase, *"the glance of the beloved,"* as a metaphor for how love affects us. Sometimes the blossoming of a flower can seem to be a response to our longing for spring. It creates beauty that we relate to emotionally.

The first time I saw Rembrandt's portrait of *An old man in military costume*, I was amazed to see how the Dutch master had created such beauty from an ordinary face of a not-so-pleasant-looking old man. After that experience, I was seeing my grandmother's face in a completely different way! Her old and wrinkled face became an interesting and very beautiful image to me. From then on, my eyes were opened to a new depth in my surroundings. I grew to love looking into the darkness, for it allowed my imagination to enter the realm of bewilderment.

Observation that inspires creativity occurs when a person welcomes mysterious vision, and appreciates the process of exploring and feeling the hidden wonders of the unknown. A lover carries gems and jewels as they follow the rainbow of life, only to discover the treasure chest in the heart. The star he follows will lead him to the unlimited sea of the soul. David Hockney said, *"It is difficult to say why I decided I wanted to be an artist. Obviously, I had some facility, more than other people, but sometimes facility comes because one is more interested in looking at things, examining them, more interested in the visual world than other people are."*

Creative observation transitions into artistic perception which in turn leads to fantasy. An internal sense of fantasy is essential for expanding creativity. We have all been scolded and told not to fantasize by our teachers, parents and friends. They tell us that spending too much time in the world of our imagination could lead us into trouble as it develops a habit of self-gratification and pleasure seeking. What they don't realize is that when our attention is focused and diffused into the fantasy that is beyond self-gratification, the energy and power can initiate deep healing and physical comfort. In fact, imagination is actually the finer basis of our material existence. The images of fantasy are actually undiscovered parts of ourselves, and imagination is there to guide us toward a new expression of our reality. We orient ourselves to internal and external reality through a variety of images. Carl Jung believed that *imagination is a direct expression of the life of our own psyche.*

When we fantasize, we are open to seeing new transformative visions. This is what it is to be a visionary – to be someone who has the capability of seeing thousands of images, as possible variations of a changing reality. Each image is a catalyst for creation, the spark for new possibility.

Through observation, one becomes more capable of developing connections and bridges even between that which appears to oppose each other. Creative fantasy is like making an imaginative collage that combines actual experiences with dreams to bring forth other possibilities and make something totally new out of them.

To observe the environment creatively, begin by looking at things from a different perspective than you are used to. Try looking around you as if you were a child seeing things for the first time. Imagine you are much smaller than you actually are and see the world as an ant might see it. Develop your power of observation by imagining what it must feel like to be a character in your favorite book. Create colors for the feelings that well up inside you. Bring them into being by giving birth to a new reality!

In the movie *Dead Poet's Society* there is a scene where the teacher has the students stand on their desks to observe the classroom from a different viewpoint than they are used to seeing while sitting at their desks. The teacher invites them to seize the day and make the most of it! The tension in the story comes from those who oppose this freedom and use pressure to prevent it.

The most interesting part of observing a space from a different perspective is that it allows us to see things quite differently – even in ways that might oppose the point of view we have already formed and taken as our own. When we can see through the eyes of someone who holds a contrasting view to our own, we can move fearlessly into new territories with the open perception of eager excitement. We take the difference into ourselves, transform it, and become able to embrace those who might once have become our enemies.

A creative person is like a magician in their capacity to create incredible images and experiences from the ordinary world around them. We can make a rabbit appear in an empty hat, just like a magician, and we can disappear into a rabbit hole, like *Alice in Wonderland*. We can experience encounters with new and intriguing characters by fantasizing in a way that turns ordinary images into an inner landscape. Inspired observation can lead to artistic expression and the thrill of mastering our creative power.

POWER OF IMAGINATION

I am enough of the artist to draw freely upon my imagination.
Imagination is more important than knowledge.
Knowledge is limited.
Imagination encircles the world.

ALBERT EINSTEIN

ONE OF THE MOST VITAL aspects of creativity is imagination. This visionary playfulness is a process of continually forming something new in the mind. It is imagination that fabricates a scene, tells a story, visualizes the form of an object changing into something new, and creates an event in a new reality that did not exist in the past.

Imagination is a marvelous gift available to every human being. We can use it to compose songs, paint pictures, invent devices, design buildings, envision and create new fashion, write books and so much more. Imagination gives wings to dreams. Without it, no airplane would have ever lifted off the ground, ships would not have sailed, and man would never have walked on the moon. Without imagination, there would be no internet or personal computers, nor would people be able to talk to each other across the globe.

The ability to explore the past, envision the future, and see each situation from a new perspective is the work of imagination. We can imagine traveling somewhere faster than the speed of light. Imagination can free us from obsessive concerns and fears, allow us to take a break from overwhelming challenges, and enable us to leave unpleasant situations for a while. Even if the reprieve we create in our minds is only temporary, it can relieve the tension that builds in the harshness of reality, bring hope and keep us going. Contrary to the belief of realists, a strong imagination does not prevent anyone from functioning in the world. It actually strengthens our ability to meet new challenges, respond to a changing environment and to empathize with others.

Imagination has a meaningful place and value in everyone's life. It utilizes the five external senses to awaken inner senses, develop a new awareness and to heighten sensations. We use it every day at work and in our playfulness without even thinking about it. It is used in conversation, in cooking, or in seeking solutions to problems. Through imagination, we can even change the way we see ourselves. Motivational speakers place great emphasis on how one can attract new opportunities into his life by visualizing possibilities.

Imagination is a power that reaches beyond creative visualization or positive thinking. It can open a portal to a new way of being in the world. It allows us to change our belief system and to experience feelings we have never felt before. Through imagination we can find a different kind of success that nurtures our being and allows us to be true to our natures instead of simply meeting the expectations others have for us.

So many people seem to be entrapped in seeing everything from a negative perspective. They expect the worst, and when they fail at something, they blame others for what happened to them. In many situations, it is the inability to utilize the power of imagination that leaves a person stranded in his suffering. Imagination invites playfulness and the joy of trying something new. A person's life can be fully enriched through a change of attitude and openness to new possibilities.

Recently, I was at a party where almost everyone seemed to be having a great time. People were gathered around the swimming pool. Young and old were jumping in and out of the pool, laughing and having fun. In the middle of all that excitement, I noticed a man who was sitting quietly on a chair looking around. As I walked closer to him and he saw I was available for a conversation, he pointed at the cracks in the wall and began telling me how the building needed to be remodeled. He was looking around inquisitively and could not think of anything other than what was wrong with what he was seeing. Everyone was invited to this party to have a good time, but the man hadn't found the freedom to open to the possibility of joy. Instead, he was looking through a negative filter at what needed to be fixed.

Imagination thrives when we are playful. Without it we can remain imprisoned in the tension of constant worry and concern. Facing something new and different that is unknown to us can generate uncertainty. Our minds prefer the safety of what we already know and fear is the catalyst that calls out the phantoms and demons that don't fit in with our rational views. But, when we live in a continual state of negative feelings and emotions, we become bound in self-imposed restrictions.

What that man at the party needed was a child to come up to him, take his hand and invite him to play. We all need that little child to guide us through the gate to remember how to have fun, to recover our lost innocence and to step into a world of playfulness and imagination. Then it becomes possible to experience something delightful and totally unexpected.

A problem many people face is that they observe themselves through a filter of scarcity. They see only what they do not possess and they project this fear of scarcity on others, dwelling on how they think others see them. They want what they do not have in the outer world and strengthen this feeling of deficiency by focusing on it and by denying the truth that exists on a deeper level within their own perception of themselves. Rumi says:

When our faith becomes all love,
we enter into greatness.
When we come from love, everything benefits,
and we live in abundance.

Creative living requires us to constantly develop our imagination by exploring many different ways of seeing. Most people are used to seeing things through curious eyes. If curiosity remains only on the surface, there will be no meaningful connection with new discoveries. In such a case, curiosity could easily cause confusion rather than the development of imagination.

People are also familiar with seeing things through inquisitive eyes, which helps us learn. Although this approach is more effective than seeing with curiosity, when we only use our rational minds it can lead us to understand things through comparison and can prevent us really seeing what is before us in a new framework.

The most effective approach to developing the imagination is to look at the environment with interest, rather than through curious or inquisitive eyes. When observation is enhanced through heightened awareness, the pathway is opened to the creation energy that is flowing through the universe. To be attracted and to see with great interest leads us to discover an incredible world that is seldom experienced by those who only see the outer forms.

When we observe with interest, there is much more chance of us benefitting from the joy it could bring. We loosen up and can actually feel the vibrating energy of excitement as a flowing stream that connects with our hearts and relieves the tension we may be carrying inside. Creative imagination activates the divine seed that is waiting to sprout inside us. If we can be flexible enough and remain open to change, to beauty, and to joy, we will be able to experience life as an unfolding, very much like the expansion of the petals of a blossoming flower. We lay ourselves open to experience the mystery of the universe.

I received my first set of paints and brushes from my parents on my eighth birthday. It was so exciting to me that I could not sleep for two days and nights and was continually playing and experimenting with them. After working with the brushes for a while, putting the paint on the canvas, I found I didn't like the way paint was smearing all over the paper. I didn't like the brushes because they were very coarse and felt like the hair on the tail of a horse. I enjoyed playing with the paint and experimenting with it, but the bristles were unpleasant to work with and interfered with my freedom to use the paints the way I wanted. I needed a sharp tip on the brush to paint the details but was reluctant to tell my parents as I did not want to make them feel badly about the gift.

One day I was swimming in the reflecting pool in our courtyard when a neighbor's cat sauntered by and came to the edge of the pool. I impulsively poured some water on the cat for fun. She jumped back and was stretching and shaking the water off her back. Her hair was wet, and little tufts began to stick together making points on her back. They looked like the tips of brushes I had seen a painter use for fine lines in miniature paintings. It was a personal revelation, and I could see that the hair from the back of the cat was exactly what I had to have to create the kind of brush I needed.

The next challenge was to figure out how to hold the little tufts of the cat's hair together to make a brush so it would be tight enough not to come apart. Many pigeons used to fly around and land in our courtyard. I would leave food out for them, so they would come back again. While flying about, sometimes they dropped their feathers. Some of the longer ones were eight to ten inches long. I had the idea to use them to make quills. The tip of the feather flared open, and there was a hole inside it. I used some soft hair from the cat and wrapped it to fit at the end of the quill.

Through experimenting, I discovered that the hair on the back of the neck of the cat was the best hair to use to make my special brushes. I began to rent cats for a few hours from the children in our neighborhood. On the weekends, kids would come to our door with their cats. I would examine them and use scissors to cut the finest hair for my brushes from the cats with the longest coats. I gave the owners a few coins in exchange. This way, I learned how to create my own special brushes to get the effect I wanted. This was a creative response to my brush dilemma. I know my parents would have taken me to the store and probably bought whatever brushes I wanted if I had talked to them. Instead, I invented a way to create my own brushes through the imaginative observation of a wet cat that guided me to be innovative and resourceful in my own way.

The brushes I created through this process became very useful to me. I kept discovering new ways to use them to create the effect I wanted in paint. I developed a spontaneous and inventive way to enhance the flow of the paint and create fine lines. This experience encouraged me to accommodate my needs and vision by finding new ways to enhance the creative process. It also gave another dimension to my surroundings. Making my own brushes at that early age turned me on to possible new purposes for the use of whatever was around me. My environment not only provides stimulation and subjects, but it can also provide creative tools and solutions. A brush, which was initially a tool, became something more valuable for me as it enhanced the joyful experience of painting.

Creativity is a way of living joyfully. We don't have to be professional artists to experience that joy. Many artists have created multiple works of art, and destroyed many of their creations. Johannes Brahms wrote that the greatness of an artist is not about how many works he creates, but it is about how many he has destroyed. Our job is also about letting go and surrendering to the creative process to guide the intricacy of what needs to go and what should remain.

I am fascinated with the series of canvases that Monet painted to capture the façade of the Rouen Cathedral at different times of the day and the year, and how it reflects changes in its appearance under different lighting conditions. He challenged himself to paint more than thirty canvases from the second floor of a building over thirty times, with each painting looking completely different from the others. Even though the building itself didn't change, Monet saw it differently every time. Through this challenge, he left the art and design world a very valuable lesson in observation and imagination, which echoed throughout the art of the twentieth century.

Monet's Rouen Cathedral canvases are only simple images of a façade seen in such a way that each painting captures an entirely different sensation. It is not just about the way he observed the light as some historians might say. Monet may have even viewed it as a study of light, but in presenting the exact same subject reflected in such a variety of ways, he offered us an insight into imagination. The feelings these canvases generate is an experience beyond the ways Monet physically represented the building. We learn from him that utilizing the power of imagination opens doors to new and wondrous possibilities. In a way, imagination allows our minds to become the canvas upon which we are able to paint our images, visual expressions and stories. What we hold within becomes what we express.

Although we are born to create in some ways that are similar to animals and plants, we are also born with the faculty of imagination, which distinguishes us from them. If we do not use that creative power, it will be our daily struggle to suppress our natural instincts. Conventional wisdom and our societal regulations make us believe that we need to produce repetitive and uninteresting work that is not stimulating. Our creativity is to be forsaken, and done so with pride, for the primary purpose of paying the bills. It is one of the reasons why we sometimes feel so empty. We constantly struggle to reach for happiness and fulfillment, without ever realizing that our ability to imagine and create holds the solutions which can totally change the reality of how we live.

In those rare moments when we connect with the nature of who we are, we experience what it means to be unlimited and in touch with the sensation of existing beyond time, space, dimension and form. This is when we recognize our true power and we begin to gain an ever more conscious access to it. The moment we engage in the creative process, we observe and see differently, and can't help but notice that we are gaining support from universal resources and our reality begins to change.

Creative imagination guides us to realize the possibilities of how we can embody our spirit and how we can live in this world but not be controlled by it. By utilizing the energy of positive intention, we can focus on new directions and be guided in how we use the power of imagination. If we align with the source of the great variety and supply of resources available to us, we will have access to even more creative visualization, and ultimately, we will move ever closer to a more creative way of life.

POWER OF VISUALIZATION

In my mind's eye, I visualize how a particular sight and feeling will appear on a print. If it excites me, there is a good chance it will make a good photograph. It is an intuitive sense, an ability that comes from a lot of practice.

ANSEL ADAMS

VISUALIZATION IS THE ABILITY TO perceive through imagination what it is that we want to achieve. Practicing creative visualization helps us to enhance our life by focusing our attention on a certain course, rather than moving in every direction without intention. Visualization is not about reaching a goal; rather it is about daring to follow the dream that attracts us most. It is somewhat like Huckleberry Finn sailing on a raft, following the course of the Mississippi River, open and welcome to the unknown on the journey.

Everyone has the ability to create their own dreams and fantasies without interference from others. Those who decide to follow their dreams, journey along a mysterious path, guided by love every step of the way. They activate their own inner resources to heal the obstacles that might be in the way so as they can continue the journey. When love is the guide, obstacles melt beneath love-driven feet. If a limitation is placed on how this appears, doubt begins to block the flow of their dreams.

Visualization as a means to reach a goal is actually a kind of self-hypnosis. It is a tool that has been used throughout history to stimulate healing. Unfortunately, there are many people who think they can reach their goals through visualization alone, without any personal effort to follow the clues or participation in discerning how love is leading them. This misunderstanding tends to make people inattentive and can lead to disappointment and feelings of failure. When things don't happen as we dreamed, it can easily lead to depression and loss of energy. However, the confusion comes when the power is believed to be outside of oneself. Believing that visualization is the agency that will bring a certain reality closer, means one can easily miss the clues, especially as you tend to come across those clues by being a creative, active participant in your life story. In the process, we learn how to trust the guidance of our inner vision and awareness.

The perception of reality is created through patterns of repetitive actions and responses that condition an individual's behavior. Our life experiences are given form through dreams and accomplishments and can generate feelings that produce a physical response. For example, when someone we love arrives unexpectedly, we feel a rush of joy in response to their appearance. This comes from our emotional conditioning.

Visualization utilizes positive images to produce positive emotions, which in turn manifest as physical sensations such as the ecstasy and the excitement we feel when we are in love. Imagine that you want to cross a stream on a foggy day. The fog is so thick that you can hardly see anything beyond your own feet. You notice a rock that is a stepping stone to take you to the other side. There is such a heavy veil of fog over the stream that it makes it difficult to see beyond the rock to know where to take the next step. You don't know how many rocks are actually there, and you have no idea where they go. This is a time when you might take a chance to visualize ways to cross the stream. The only way to cross the stream is to move ahead into the unknown in uncertainty. As we take each step and another rock appears we develop faith in the process of visualization and feel more confident in turning to our inner senses for guidance.

You step out into the unknown onto the first stone, and it is only then that you can see the next one through the fog. You surrender to the flow of this action that guides you from one step to the next. In the flow, there is a play between what one envisions and how one actually moves to take an action. One grows into the visualization through the attraction and the guidance to move which is very similar to the pull of gravity on the tides of the ocean.

We have been warned to stay away from trusting this process, because it can turn into fantasy, obsession and delusion. Yet, when we are awakened by the longing for the light, and love is our muse, we learn to trust that the stone will be right where it needs to be to keep us from falling in the stream. We develop faith in what we cannot see with our outer eyes. This kind of creative visualization is quite different from the trivial images and suggestive words the world often attaches to the idea of discovery. Envisioning a creative solution can be a very positive help in following a path in life.

The creative result can only emerge when we surrender to something that has proven itself, given us faith and set love as our guiding star. It is our muse, our one pure guide toward reality, and something leaps within us in recognition when it comes. When we step into the stream, we can imagine we are holding an invisible hand that guides us to the next stone, and we know that we will be led in the way that is right for us. This awareness helps us to move freely without knowing where to step in order to reach the next stone. Of course, this kind of visualization and risk is created in balance with our faith and the capacity to handle it.

When our dreams and desires evolve from a continuing cycle that is trusted and recognized, they are easy to follow. If they are not trusted and seem unreal, they turn into a negative action that can destroy what might have otherwise been possible. As an example, if while I am painting a serene seen, suddenly I hear a disturbing loud sound, my creative flow comes to a halt and, in most cases, unexpected changes take place. This is not meant to be a judgment, because the negative reaction is not necessarily a bad thing, nor is it an immoral action. It is a movement that destroys the unnecessary elements that appear in the visualization that are not really needed to achieve the result. This is true in our own behavior, in our relationships, as it is in most everything we create. A strong faith and the creative power of visualization are needed for dreams to be realized.

Every time I stand in front of a canvas to begin a new painting, I am excited about developing images that are not yet known to me in any conscious way. I dream, imagine and try to envision other dimensions that have not been apparent in my immediate and surrounding reality. Sometimes while I paint, I visualize myself traveling through a different dimension where I encounter something beyond my ordinary experiences. Other times, I imagine I am only one inch tall, and envision myself walking through the forms and colors in my paintings experiencing a world that is quite unlike what I actually know.

I constantly change scales to create for the fun and excitement of it. One might say I dip my brush in the collective unconscious, the sea that harbors the energy of all that has ever been created, and all that is yet to be created. Yet, I am immersed in the present moment of what is reaching to come through me, all of it pooling in my human incarnation to reveal the face of something new. It is energizing, and being a part of this birthing process generates a feeling of being fully alive.

As I continue playing with paint on the canvas, some stepping stones appear out of the fog. Those are the images that attract me as they seem to appear through my playfulness. At this point, I need to choose the image or several images that I would like to develop further. It is like finding the strongest stone that I can use as a footstep to cross the stream. That becomes a decision, in which I visualize what the developed image might look like before I take the next step. I set my direction, built on the momentum of the assumption that the image is something I would like to create, just as certain stones form the path to take me across the stream.

As long as I am not finding any image on the canvas that excites me, I keep on playing in total freedom. When I see images that I like, the movement makes a shift. My visualization begins to develop, and my playfulness finds a direction. As I continue painting, I then move forward with confidence in my capability to carry my vision through to completion. If I don't experience the physical result in some way, I lose the value of the visualization, and I don't know what to look for – much like not being able to find the next stepping stone through the fog and falling in the stream. It is like having a fantasy for which I have created no foundation.

When something appears on the canvas, my entire intention is to eliminate whatever is blocking the clarity of the appearing forms. My brush moves on the canvas to eliminate the extras, following my visualization to intuit which image is to be removed or hidden. In each instance, there is a decision to save something and a decision to eliminate; one is positive and the other is negative. I will take either this direction or that direction, without giving them any emotional value. The flow will guide me in that action. It is in this moment that I freely surrender to my inner guidance. This is how the visualization becomes a reality and how my choices guide me to finish the painting.

The decision to keep or to eliminate an image is determined by surrendering to the movement of the creative flow itself. Most artists create something new in the free state of bewilderment and eliminate through the rational mind. While creating, a person is surrendered to the creative flow; when eliminating, they follow the visualization. When we surrender to the flow, creation takes place without hesitation, because we have already visualized it in the mind. This does not come about through any fixed or predetermined destiny that is *absolute* in its nature. We are not moving toward any outer object or goal when we are in the process of creating or in the movement of life itself.

When we engage in this new way of being, our upbringing, our beliefs, our culture, and our values are involved in how we perceive and participate. We compare and evaluate what is happening in light of who we are and what our past experiences have been. This usually prevents us from limiting or preventing our surrender into the new experience. This happens quite often to most artists while they are creating. When I discover a form that I recognize on my canvas, it is based on my own personal knowledge of form, and my past experience wields a strong influence to help guide me with the images I am painting.

When I reach the point where I am dealing with a recognizable image, suddenly my joyful journey of discovery comes to a halt, and my flight into the imagination is grounded. I connect with something in the past, and that freezes the flow of new possibilities. Comparison is inevitable, and then I become judgmental about what I am painting. I begin looking for a standard that I accept and trust according to my values or beliefs. Once that happens, I am trapped in it. I become enslaved to developing the form in a familiar way. I am locked into a comparison of my own expectations from the past.

Creating through comparison is like being caught in a web of insignificant detail. I can use a great deal of time and energy to find the way through it whenever it catches me. To free myself from this web of details binding me in time, I often turn the canvas around to obscure the familiar images, until I become attracted to something else that allows my focus to move in a different direction, away from what is recognizable in conventional forms. I follow my perceptiveness, rather than my skills of observation. Perception becomes the attracting influence that guides me. By having the intention of being open to the unknown, I am able to create a new path to follow. I move beyond my own resistance to the unknown and take a risk to surrender to the excitement and seductiveness of the invisible.

We observe the familiar with our outer eyes as we look around at what is outside of us. We perceive something new and unfamiliar when we withdraw our outward attention and look inward. We attend to the inner vision that is mysteriously developing within us.

One of my childhood experiences that had a great impact in developing my commitment to a creative flow was my relationship with an old musician whose name was Yavari. Knowing him and spending time with him helped me to recognize and develop my own perception. Yavari was blind. His eyes were open, but he could not see the outer forms. The entire inside of his eyes were red. He played an instrument called a *ney*, which is one of the oldest wind instruments still in use. It is a hollow cane or a reed with five or six finger holes and one hole for the thumb.

Yavari was a virtuoso performer on the ney in his youth, but as the instrument lost its popularity, he was forced to live in poor conditions in his old age. He collected money from some of his former fans to survive living in a basement room, which looked like a place for underground storage purposes. I came to know this old master through my uncle, and I was attracted to him at first as someone who would be a good subject for me to paint. Since his basement room was not far from my house, I used to go see him after school with a sketch pad and watercolors, and I would always bring some food and money for him. Every time he heard my steps coming down the stairs, he knew it was me by the sound. He was usually sitting on a pillow leaning back against the cement wall playing his ney.

The sound of Yavari's reed flute was magical to me, but what I came to enjoy the most was listening to him tell me of his life. His stories were very surreal to me at that age, because they were often created from inner visions. My enthusiasm for his stories would excite him and motivate him to tell them in colorful and creative ways. The stories of this man, who was blind to the outside world, were narratives of the heart, and they were filled with inspiring imagery for me. I was often painting while listening to him. Sometimes, he would laugh like a child, other times tears would be falling from those open and reddened eyes as he would describe his feelings to me.

One of his stories was about a time when he picked up his reed flute early in the morning and made his way up the steps to the street and began playing while walking down the middle of the road. He said the sound of his flute was so exciting that young girls and women were coming to their open windows and out onto the balconies by the thousands, and they were showering him with roses. He played and walked along the streets on a carpet of roses, and pedestrians, who had gathered along the road, were crying with joy as they listened to his music.

I knew that the old master was not even capable of leaving the dungeon where he was confined and forced to live, but his perception and imagination was giving him eyes to see the people he described, and he was able to connect with the hearts of the thousands of lovers in his dream. Every time he played his instrument as he visualized himself in that state, he was truly creating music of love through his heart.

I went to Yavari's basement room for several years, until one day he was found dead, gone forever from this world. Yet, his vision and perception stayed alive within me and was later reflected in many of my paintings. Even now, after all the years that have passed, his vision sometimes comes to me while I am painting, and I enter into a dream world of perception that obliterates any rational thought that would limit my vision.

Through those valuable moments with Yavari, I learned to allow my perception to guide me, not only on the canvas, but in many other aspects of my life. The most important thing I learned from the blind master was that I could access a timeless world of vision with my eyes closed, and I could perceive what was in my heart much more clearly than I could ever do with my eyes open.

When we do not place any limitation on our dreams or desires, we save them from being lost to doubt. Doubt is the result of an experience that we envision through our mind, whether it is real or imagined, and we become anxious about our capability to see it develop. It flaunts the possibility of failure before us to undermine our positive faith in living our dream. This can easily turn into a hallucination and eventually could become an obsession. We become obsessed with doing when we are without a dream, living in the repetitive motion of meaningless activity.

The visualization process goes through three developing stages. The first stage is observing what is around us through the use of our five external senses. During the second stage, our brain takes into process whatever we have experienced externally. Then we feel the interplay of the influence of our culture, our traditions, and our past experiences having an effect on the interpretation of what we visualize. If what we observe does not have some corresponding support in our memory, it is unlikely to develop any further.

During the third stage, we react to the experience and form an impression. If what enters our mind has no connection with our past experience, it is unlikely that we will perceive it in any meaningful way. When we see something that is familiar to us, our rational mind sees it as real, whether it exists or not. In looking at an abstract painting, our mind searches for something that we can recognize, and what is closest to our past experience becomes what we can see and comprehend. The reason many motivational speakers tell us that we create our own reality is because we can reflect only on what we know and have experienced in the past.

Visualization is very influential in the creative process. Without perceiving, whatever we create would lack guidance, and if perception does not lead to creation, it serves no resourceful purpose. Perception and creation are two sides of the same coin, two processes that are intricately related, each one enhancing and expanding the other.

Throughout history, there were many creative men and women who could capture their powerful visualizations directly into their works. They were the visionaries who saw into the future. Many artists are considered visionaries because of the type of works they have created. There were also visionaries who had a clear, distinctive and specific vision of the future in technology, and in the social or political arena.

Visionaries start by visualizing what they want to create. Architects, designers and great inventors have used visualization as the first step in their creations. They visualized each work before they ever put anything on paper. Most visionaries tell us that they love to use their imagination, for that is what develops the capability to visualize.

Einstein used visualization techniques to arrive at some of his theories. He came to his theory of relativity by visualizing what the world would look like if he rode through the universe on a beam of light. Visualization was his preferred method of discovery, and he often recommended it to his students.

Many creative people would say that they have carried the visions from their journals for a long time, and the pages have been scattered around their love nests like wildflowers. Those lovers have learned how to open their hearts to become the ones who can receive and carry the visions that flow out to others. Their visions are like fountains flowing with the clear water of truth that is meant for everyone. They have learned how to be receivers of a greatness we cannot really name or even speak aloud, because it is always changing and expanding, dancing and spinning, and pouring out a stream of the 'stuff' of creation. This is the essence of life that wants to be known, expressed and manifested in a way only the heart can help us achieve. This is the mystery attracting us and drawing us into a more exalted life.

Visionaries do this by unlearning and eliminating all that blocks them from listening for and hearing the precious messages of inspiration, and clearing the way for experiences of awe and wonder. They learn what it means to behold what they see, to receive what the great unknown is whispering to them. It is like spring when everything opens and reveals what it has been created to be without needing to name or receive any credit for it. Each manifestation just opens and blossoms in its own unique way and shines out like the sun for everyone.

When we submit to the power of visualization, we plunge ourselves into a silence so quiet that we can hear our heart beating. We can hear the excited whispering of our heart. A hush comes over us, surrounds us, and we can hear our lifeblood rushing through our bodies.

When we feel that joy, and we experience the sensation that fills our being, we realize we had forgotten the whispering lips of this great lover, because we were surrounded by too much noise, both in the outside world and circling inside our heads. All this noise can be frightening, and we tend to turn on even more noise to drown out the unfamiliar. We forget what it means to run to this greatness that is always and ever seeking our peace and wellbeing, and longs to show us revelations of wonder as new expressions of the infinite ways love comes to us.

In the creative process, it is not so important to understand how this works on a mental level, for it is guided through us on a feeling level that we learn to recognize by remembering the innocent, trusting joy of childhood play. Creativity encompasses a heritage that is beyond what we can describe. This journey is highly unique and personal to each one of us, which is why judgment has no place in the creative process.

Through creative action, we learn to honor the gaze of our beloved that we see through the eyes of love. Out of the unseen, love grants us a vision that we have somehow been prepared to express. This grace calls for the highest integrity and we respond by being as true to its expression as we are able to be. We are privileged to honor and share this truth.

If our outer experience of life has not given us a glimpse of this purity, or we have lost our faith in the beauty of a love that is not self-seeking, then visualization can grant us a glimpse of this presence within us through an unexplainable grace.

Joseph Campbell gave us many wonderful accounts of how this loving presence arises within to befriend us, across cultures and time, through our rituals and traditions, our dances and music, and beyond place and belief systems. This can equally happen to the shaman dancing around the fire, the artist lying on his back painting images of creation on the ceiling of a church, or the musician hearing the fullness of an aria in the silences within him.

According to Campbell, a positive, literal belief in the mythological sphere follows spiritual experience, not the other way around. He believed:

> *Mythology is thus of a kind with the formal arts; music, architecture, and the dance; poetry and the visual arts. For the arts, when properly turned, yield an impact of experience – not logical reference to known or unknown facts or ideas. The art of art consists, in fact, in the presentation of forms, images or ideas in such a way that they will constitute an order of spiritual fulfillment.*

To be open to the experience, we must first suspend our doubt. We need to put our disbelief aside, just long enough to take the first steps into the spiritual experience of visualization. However it comes to us, it is healing to our negative experiences and comforting to our fears. It is not up to us to judge what brings about this experience in our own hearts or in the hearts of our fellow human beings.

The goal of comparative studies of religion is not to name the right one or the one that is true for everyone. Studying different religions can help us discover the creative power through which healing and love and joy come to each one of us. For some it comes in a group experience, for some it comes when alone, and the form it takes in our lives is a sacred event that we have long failed to recognize. It is time for us to affirm the journey of the seeker and rediscover the path of this lived expression, rather than criticize or negate the holiness of love's expression within us.

Creative power comes through a visualizing process that silently forms before our eyes. Our hands, eyes and hearts gratefully surrender to the guiding energy to bring its visions into being. Feelings are transformed into colors and movements that sweep across the canvas like the gentle breeze of morning, or mysteriously show up as images in the shadows and subtle contrasting shades and forms we cannot even explain. Sometimes faces appear that seem to create themselves. We stand amazed at what is expressed through us, and someone asks us what it means, and we can only answer that we don't know.

We are like buds wrapped in layers of wonderful secrets that want to whisper to us, but we can become afraid of this kind of tenderness and beauty. We are afraid to open in case we find that nothing is there. We need warmth, silence and faith to trust the greatness already circling around us, inviting us to bloom and sip the dew that forms on the open petals of every flower.

Visualization is not just for a few talented people. It is for everyone. It is not about talent, but about tapping into the gift of creation itself, the energy of love that moves the universe. This is the spin that keeps it spinning. This is the resurrecting creative power that creates an infinite variety of faces, forms and dreams that we cannot even imagine.

POWER OF INTUITION

Intuition is the key to everything, in painting, filmmaking, business - everything. I think you could have an intellectual ability, but if you can sharpen your intuition, which they say is emotion and intellect joining together, then a knowingness occurs.

DAVID LYNCH

INTUITION IS THE DIRECT INNER knowledge or perception of something without mental reasoning or the conscious use of thought. It is different from insight, which is the ability to understand the nature of things, whether they exist, or not.

Intuition has an aura of mystery around it, like seeing into a crystal ball, or the way the illusion of magic is experienced, which is something that cannot be fully understood. It is a mythical concept that has been called witchcraft or described as the skill of fortune tellers. Perception is a power that most scientific minds do not accept, because it can't be researched or proven in any definitive way. But, the heart does not seek proof, for it is affirmed in the flood of assurance that awakens it to the inner mysteries.

Intuition lights the way in the creative process. It is different from an outer light, such as a streetlight, that casts its glow around itself in a circling arc. The guiding light is more like a flashlight that is carried in hands, focusing a beam and pointing the way to follow. Many people are not aware of this hidden aspect of creativity, at least not in a conscious way. We tap into the intuitive power, tune into it, push against it, and like a piñata, when we strike it, it breaks open and the sweetness of surprise comes tumbling out.

Intuition is the fountainhead of creative inspiration, the source from which insight originates. It will guide us to solutions for most internal and external problems and to face challenges that come to us along the way. We intuit the reactions of others in a way that enhances our creative process and enables us to carry it through. Through intuition, we bring what we have received in the past into the present to create the future. It reveals itself in a flash of insight, which is sometimes called a gut feeling.

Our intuition has an innate awareness of the connection between the present moment and what happens next. It is an embracing energy that seems to know us better than we know ourselves. It senses the state of our present condition and responds instantly to the inner questions and concerns we are facing. Above all, intuition is the power that develops imagination.

When Picasso was asked whether ideas come to him by chance or by design, he responded, *"I don't have a clue. Ideas are simply starting points. I can rarely set them down as they come to my mind. As soon as I start to work, others well up in my pen. To know what you're going to draw, you have to begin drawing. Every time I find myself facing a blank page, I simply begin. What I capture in spite of myself interests me more than my own ideas."*

Even for a great scientist like Albert Einstein, insight did not come from logic or mathematics. It came from his intuition and inspiration. He said, *"When I examine myself and my methods of thought, I come close to the conclusion that the gift of imagination has meant more to me than any talent for absorbing absolute knowledge. At times I feel certain I am right while not knowing the reason."*

Mystics recognize intuition as a mystery and don't concern themselves too much with defining it. It is the energy that surrenders to a divine justice inherent in life. Sufis see intuition in two different ways and from two different perspectives. One is a way of looking – a divine way of seeing through the eyes. The other way is embedded within us. It is already ours, and we align with the power as we awaken to it. No matter how the realization comes, there is an aura of mystery that surrounds it.

> *If you are not my soul, kindred spirit is useless to me!*
> *If you don't offer me intuition, insight is not what I want!*
> *I have never been able to create anything but your reflection!*
> *When you don't attract me into the flow,*
> *creativity is not what I want!*
>
> RUMI

Artists, poets, and prophets are often intuitive, which means they can know and sense things beyond the barriers of time, and space, and the ordinary boundaries that prevent our seeing. Their primary concern is with possibilities, which depend on the artist remaining open to them. Everyone with intuition is able to sense and feel what is invisible and not perceptible to the ordinary eye. Such a person is given a glimpse of wholeness, in a similar way that a flash of lightning suddenly illuminates something in the dark the moment it strikes.

My own artistic life was guided by my intuitive nature, although for a long time I thought it was coincidence. One of my first memories of intuition relates to when I was ten years old. During a summer break, my mother took me to visit her cousin in Tehran. On the last day of the trip, she took me to a store to buy a pair of shoes for herself. While the shopkeeper was fitting shoes on her, I noticed an open door at the far end of the store. Without any concern, I got up and wandered through the door into a room, which looked like a bookstore in the back of the shoe store. There was an older man sitting behind a table that was covered with piles of book.

As I walked toward the table, an open book with colored pictures caught my attention. I asked the man if I could have the book. He told me I needed to buy it. I ran back to the shoe store and told my mother that I found a book in the other room, which I really wanted to have. She said she had no more money. I broke into tears and cried and pleaded until my mother gave up buying the shoes and bought the book for me.

The book was a painting catalogue of several Russian artists, including Repin, Aivazovsky, and Shiskin. The images were printed in full color. That book became my prized possession and my portal to the art world. I kept it near me wherever I was, even as I slept. At night, I placed the book under my pillow. I copied many of the paintings in that book, which made me familiar with the European style of painting. Looking back, I realize I was intuitively guided to go with my mother on that trip as it initiated the entire course of my creative life.

For an intuitive person, creative power follows visualization. Clues guide the way, and they become instinctively recognized. It is crucial to stay alert to the clues, for when we are lost or confused, something in us still remembers and is holding the energy of the memory, so we can surrender to that power and follow its guiding light. Eventually, we develop a relationship with that inner light, which we sometimes call our muse.

To turn away from intuitive feelings, is to lose a very precious resource, for it is like having a freeway to follow, a path of intuition that has no median or shoulder. We keep moving, for if we don't, others will push us out of the way. The more we remain open, the more we learn to accept and recognize the power it gives us, and the more capable and aware we become. When we tune into our intuition, we are aware of its guiding influence, in much the same way as a person who is dieting has an inner awareness of their intention to lose weight.

The creative power of intuition is developed more easily in a joyful environment. If someone feels pressured or is experiencing pain or grief, it is much more difficult to tune into the discerning perception that guides the way. Sometimes the intuition of friends, who know us well, can give us insight into our own behavior during those difficult times.

Rational thinking often works against intuition, because when we try to determine a response or an action with the mind, reason alone does not give us the insight we need to make a decision. We need the guidance of intuition to light the way in the darkness of our unknowing. In order to develop that intuitiveness, we need to align with our deeper instincts rather than spending time thinking about things too much. The deep feeling of weariness comes to those who fall into a repetitive cycle of thinking and mulling things over and over.

If we do something creative, like painting, dancing, building castles in the sand, or anything out of the ordinary that lets us be spontaneous, we develop the freedom to feel. Unfortunately, when we are worried and concerned about something, we don't think of it as a time to go out and have fun. Yet, it may be exactly what we need to find our balance. Laughter can have great healing power when it comes from joy!

Intuition is not wishful thinking. It is quite a different experience. It flows from a deeper source that has stored the collective responses of a lifetime – physically, emotionally, and spiritually. The path of creativity invites us to grow and develop according to our capabilities. We use our intuitive perception in ways that enrich the experiences of both ordinary and very special moments. It is a path of grace, and we are quite fortunate when we are blessed by its presence. Sufis speak of it as when the 'Friend' comes to be with us. Intuition can be the movement of befriending ourselves in any number of ways!

Listening to our intuition is the essence and real value of art and creativity. Supposedly, when Michelangelo was asked how he created the statue of David, the most renowned sculpture in the world, from a block of stone, he replied that he did not create David from the stone; rather that David was already in the stone, and he merely chipped away the unnecessary parts until David emerged. What most people do not know is that on hearing this, one of his apprentices asked Michelangelo how he knew that David was in the stone. The master answered in one word, *intelleto*, which means in English something equivalent to divine intellect, or what is called intuition. It is inner knowing that prompts us to reach for something that wants to be known.

Intuition is what most artists utilize to develop their artworks. Once we awaken our inner guide by unlocking what Michelangelo called *intelleto*, or the wisdom of our subconscious mind, we already intrinsically know what to do next. Being objective is much more difficult, because when we are truly creating, we only have the awareness of our emotions. That is the reason the work of art generates more interest when artists utilize their emotions as an influence rather than trying to express the ideas through their rational minds. We may be impressed by their intelligence or talent, but we are more likely to be moved by their emotions!

When a work of art is created intuitively, it communicates through symbols, colors and forms that trigger feelings and emotions within us. It doesn't appear to us in cleverly delineated forms, but we do have the intuition to perceive the guidance of passionate feelings.

As an internal sense, intuition may not be as quick as intellect to access information, but it is deeper in its insight. Intuition does not help us grasp things as easily as the intellect, which is able to recognize certain situations and behaviors as a series of complex operations and behavioral responses. Yet, intuition can help us grasp how these relate to each other and help us make meaningful connections with ourselves and others. When we think we understand, intuition tends to make connections that at first appear to be of little value, because thinking instinctively tries to dominate our deeper feelings and desires. It easily makes connections we may have otherwise brushed off as having little meaning or relevance to our journey.

Intuition can be developed and strengthened through practice in the same way as exercise develops muscles. Learning to listen to the inner voice can tone and strengthen intuitive powers. When gut instincts are ignored and the gift of intuition is not used, we are making a choice to limit our possibilities. Instead, we tend to over analyze and over think what concerns us. Our intuitive ability slips out of sight, because we are not using or trusting it.

My own experience continues to show me that the more I pay attention to this inner power, the more creative my choices are, and the more joyful my life becomes. The whispering guidance of the 'Friend,' that I was introduced to as a child through the intuitive kindness of the mystics, continues to be relentlessly with me. There are times we all wish we had that kind of 'Friend' when we really need one. That 'Friend' only shows up when we recognize intuition as a compassionate presence and sacred insight.

POWER OF INSPIRATION

Write down the thoughts of the moment.
Those that come unsought for are commonly the most valuable.

FRANCIS BACON

INSPIRATION IS THE CATALYST THAT lights the fire or sets the journey of creativity in motion. Without it, there would be no work of art or scientific discovery. In fact, very little that is new and creative would come into the world. Inspiration gives us the means of reaching the mystery beyond our worldly identities. Surrendering to inspiration brings about a greatness that is the glory of existence.

Like a kiss, inspiration opens the heart to receive the spiraling, creative grace that lovingly flows through the universe. Lack of inspiration is the most common problem faced by anyone trying to create something, regardless of the subject or level of experience. Some suffer from it more often than others, but there is no avoiding it.

Traditionally, inspiration has been defined as a subconscious burst of creativity in an artistic endeavor. It is found in both Greek and Hebrew literature to mean 'breathed upon by God.' Ancient religions considered it a divine matter. In Christianity, inspiration is a gift of the Holy Spirit. In the *Book of Amos*, the prophet describes being overwhelmed by God's voice and compelled to speak.

Sufis connect inspiration to someone's embodiment of God's attributes, by entering a state of ecstasy or a kind of divine madness, beyond control of the mind. Romantic poets believed that inspiration came to them because their soul was able to receive such visions. In all cases, inspiration is viewed as being beyond the direct control of a person.

In modern psychology, inspiration is seen as an entirely internal process. Sigmund Freud believed it comes from the inner psyche of the artist, directly from the subconscious. Surrealist artists explored this concept of inspiration by turning to dream diaries and automatic writing, to try to tap into what they considered to be the true source of art.

Inspiration has nothing to do with the skill or capability of an individual, and therefore, it is possible for anyone to be inspired. Sometimes, the most skilled of artists is unable to be inspired. Inspiration differs from revelation, which is a conscious process, where the one creating is aware and interacting with the vision. Inspiration can be felt without complete understanding.

The flow of inspiration comes through the heart, which is the creative regenerative power that can move it in countless ways and be expressed in a unique way in each life form. Longing is the powerful driver of this process that gives rise to creation. It prepares the way for a vision that wants to rise out of what is unknown to become known. At its deepest level, it is a longing to create. In this way, the longing for sunlight is the inspiration for a plant to grow.

Inspiration refers to moments of bewilderment, a kind of sweet madness that expands a vision toward the infinite. Spinning in it can create and manifest joy. Geniuses are those who allow the breath of God to be continually expressed through them. Picasso was constantly inspired by just about everything he could see or feel. That is what guided him to create nearly sixteen thousand paintings and drawings, in addition to his sculptures and ceramics.

Inspiration is a mindless energy that seeks to express itself. It is a moment when a unique sensation enters the heart, and a creative power moves to give it form. We sometimes call it incarnation. It is an experience of abundance, an overflowing of sensory pleasure. When that positive charge of energy is felt in the heart, an aura of sweetness surrounds us, and we create because it is our nature to create. In that moment, we fall into a pure stream of creative power. Khalil Gibran described it as the moment when *the earth delights to feel your bare feet and the wind longs to play with your hair.*

Throughout our lives, we face so many problems and challenges that we feel incapable of solving, and we are forced to face our limitations. Yet, concealed in the obstacles, are hidden solutions. We harbor a potential and strength that we have yet to discover. Inspiration helps us to tap the source of that power to encounter and experience the indwelling mystery within us. When our purpose is to give birth to our ideal self, inspiration allows us to see ourselves in a new way every time.

Close your eyes for a minute and try to remember a silence so quiet that you can hear and feel your heart beating. The swishing, whispering sound of the blood moving through your body, is an intimate sound, like the breathing of a lover. When you breathe into this memory, the sensation that comes over you and fills your being is very much like the feeling of inspiration. This precious whispering sound can easily be forgotten when we are surrounded by the harsh noises of the world and by the internal noise of our own thoughts.

All the artistic expression of my life is the result of an inspiring moment in my early teens. One summer while I was going to junior high school my parents took me to the city of Mashhad by train. The ride took almost two days and one night. Early in the morning of the second day, I was standing in line waiting to use the washroom, watching the orange sky of the early morning. Just as the sun was appearing in the horizon, a young, teenage girl in a thin, blue, transparent nightgown suddenly walked into my view.

She blended with the sunrise for a short moment, and that image registered in my heart forever. The silhouette of her body beneath that thin gown against the golden rays of the sun is unforgettable to me. In that moment, it felt as if lightning moved through me, and I began to tremble with emotion.

A moment later, the girl was gone, and I never saw her again. Yet, the image I saw on the train that morning became a glorious, visual inspiration throughout my life. I have been inspired to paint that image in so many variations. It is an archetype, an image of beauty from the collective unconscious that still, after all those years, arouses desire and longing in my soul.

Inspiration is a flashing moment. We have no knowledge of what will happen next. We can't plan for it. We can only surrender to it. We need to drop all predetermined notions of what might happen next. Just like the silhouette of the girl on the train, inspiration is a gift of the moment, like the kiss that we remember forever, but cannot hold on to. It writes itself upon our hearts. It is an impression that is embraced by the heart and happens unexpectedly, like a flash of lightning, and then it is gone.

The act of creation is triggered by inspiration. If that spark is carried beyond the moment, we may try to control the creative process by comparing the moment to something that is recognizable to us. Mentally, we seek to analyze it by turning to what is familiar. Inspiration that lasts beyond the flashing moment may even create a block in the creative process. We need to surrender, stay open, and be aware of the creative flow to feel the inspiration of life moment by moment.

Inspiration usually recreates itself to guide the creative process. It unfolds moment by moment in the creative flow. Inspiration is a gift, like receiving a key to the gates of Heaven. If we turn away from it, the door might close and be locked to us. We develop a faith in our intuitive gifts as they are revealed to us.

The creative leap that helps us transcend our limitations is mostly triggered by what inspires us. It can turn our need into surplus, our scarcity into abundance, our weakness into power, and our pain into remedy. When we are inspired, a light turns on inside of us, and we glow with new ideas. This radiance shines out from us as a diffusion of energy that lights the way for others in the dark. Rumi tells us how we can nurture the power of inspiration by transcending our limitations. He says:

The sound of the bow provokes fear
for the arrow wounds its mark.
What is sensed beyond the unseen
is inspired by perception.
Increase your necessity
to increase your perception.

Inspiration moves beyond religion, beyond tradition, beyond conventional wisdom, and allows love to become the divine inspiration that brings us together in the joy of creating. It is inspiration that allows us to share in the freedom of the life force of the creator within each one of us. We are meant to be messengers of the light, to radiate and share its graces for the benefit of everyone. Compassion and courage create ripples that flow out from our kindness to others and lift the veil of darkness to help us know that we are not alone.

As we are inspired, we make a shift to balance the opposing energies within us. It is like a pendulum. We touch into the darkness and the light, the sound and the silence, and we find the centering stream of love that keeps us moving. We allow the movement to feel the flow. Whether human or divine, inspiration is a connection with a higher intellect, a collective intelligence, that Michelangelo called *intelleto*. When our hearts guide us, we are free to draw from this well in order to create. If we try to create from the smallness of our rational minds, we continually bump up against all of our limitations.

Our creative power is unleashed when we are able to utilize all that we are to fuse with the present moment and enter the timelessness of a new dimension. We draw on the gifts of our upbringing, pooling the past and the future into the present, and we trust the rhythm that flows through us. We are inspired by the vision and we transcend the limits of time as we follow our hearts. Sometimes we are inspired by others, and other times, we follow our own heart. If we follow the path set by someone else, we are guided by their rules and beliefs, and can try them on to see how it feels. When we follow our own heart, we fall into the ecstasy of the flow of creative power.

Time flows in all directions in the multi-dimensional realm of mystery. We coax and entice the beauty to bring it to life on canvas, in poetry, in music, through touch, or by creating something that becomes a reflection of our inspiration. This is the wholeness appearing through the creative process. In one moment we have inspiration, and in the next a vision appears or music fills the air with a song that breaks free from the heart! Then as 'artists' we develop the inspiration in the most creative way we know. Bob Marley described this so profoundly when he said, *"I have no education. I have inspiration. If I were educated, I would be a damn fool."*

When the mysterious feeling of inspiration prompts us, we welcome and savor the unveiling process that invites us to express it. If we cling to the rules and beliefs of others, we stifle the outpourings of our own hearts. We need to shed the covering that lets us hide beneath it. When we shed our disguises, love becomes our protector and we relax into the flow of its guidance.

Many of the best works of art often happen in a very short period of time. It is interesting to observe how the sketches and drawings of many artists are often more powerful than their finished paintings. The early workings can capture the inspiration that guides the completed work. It is a manifestation of the moment, a glimpse of something, that leads to the finished work. By not laboring over something too long, freedom guides the expression. I often compare it to how we express love in relationship, for the best moments of lovemaking happen when we allow the flow. We surrender to our desire and let the freedom of expression and the energy of love guide what happens.

INSPIRATION AND MOTIVATION

One of the common mistakes we make is confusing inspiration with motivation and treating them as if they are synonymous. There is a major difference between the two. Inspiration connects with the heart to activate the creative process. Motivation connects with the mind, is often ego driven, and moves us toward accomplishing something. For example, if we are motivated to earn an adequate income to support our family, we may try some work or a new approach to get the result that we want. Being motivated does move and activate the mind, but it can also leave us in doubt and anxiety. Motivation brings us into a gray area in which we want to do so much, but are too busy to be inspired by anything. It is a space of action and planning, so we leave the feelings and desires of the heart behind.

We tend to become motivated when we are persuaded to do something to make us more successful. I remember working with an art publisher who handled the sales of my artworks. The program was quite encouraging for me economically, and I was becoming comfortable with it. One day, when I was going through the images of some of my paintings, I noticed many of my more recent works were using color combinations that were different to my earlier ones. I did not feel good about this, and I didn't like the colors nearly as much as those I had used in the past.

I kept looking through my paintings to figure out the reason why I had changed my approach. Suddenly, it dawned on me that the company directors were motivating me to work with certain colors, because they were more marketable. They harmonized better with the color schemes in people's homes. There is nothing wrong with this approach, except that the motivation focused on my earning power, and I was not inspired by what I was painting at all. I could do it and make the pieces more salable, but I was losing my excitement for creating. It was a major discovery to realize that when I was simply motivated by profit or pleasing someone else, I was blocking the flow of what was truly inspiring me to create!

Inspiration is a catalyst for creativity, but motivation is more of a trigger for worldly success. When Michelangelo began to paint the ceiling of the Sistine Chapel, he was initially commissioned by the Pope to paint the twelve Apostles. This was quite a motivation and challenge for him. Not long after he started the project he became doubtful about his ability to carry the commission through. He was simply too depressed to continue, and he finally gave up the work and left the chapel and the city of Rome.

To be away from the Pope and the domain of his influence, Michelangelo moved to Sicily to return to sculpting, which was the love of his life. Sometime later, a cloud formation inspired him to paint God's finger reaching out to Adam's. Having found the inspiration to paint the image, he moved back to Rome to create what we now witness as a striking image of the creation of man – one of the most recognizable images in western culture. All the motivation that the Pope had used to engage Michelangelo had only brought him pain and frustration, while one moment of inspiration became the incentive to create one of the most profoundly inspiring works of art.

Inspiration is entirely self-generated, moved by feelings arising from within. When love makes an appearance, a lighter spirit comes forth and offers a feeling of excitement and a strong desire to act on it immediately. When I am inspired to create, I become so excited that I forget my physical needs. I just want to follow the flow of the energy moving through me. When I am in this state, it takes precedence over hunger, over my need for sleep, and over every other activity I might ordinarily be doing. I am energized, and joy is expanding my heart and spilling over into the room around me. I become gifted with an experience of paradise, and visions seem to be forming out of the great energy that I feel for what I am doing!

Others often tell me that I can create because I have time to be inspired, while they have to go to work, take their children to school, do shopping, cook meals, do laundry, pay bills, and do other mundane chores. I respond by suggesting they examine the reasons why they are not choosing to live an inspired life. Obviously, if someone continues to do what they really don't want to do, they will struggle to become inspired. If someone is doing all those things because they love their family, and because it gives them joy to do things for them, ordinary experiences can become exalted as quickly as creating works of art. When life evolves out of a feeling of doing what 'we have to do' or what 'we should do,' the experiences lose the energy of spontaneity and the exhilaration of free choice is lost.

> *I decided that it was not wisdom that enabled poets to write their poetry, but a kind of instinct or inspiration, such as you find in seers and prophets who deliver all their sublime messages without knowing in the least what they mean.*
>
> SOCRATES

Inspiration initiates a more heartfelt decision and effort that makes a connection with the emotions evolving from love. Motivation is based on some persuasive rules, consequences, and sometimes, by the use of force, and we can end up feeling like a slave.

When I feel inspired to paint, I create with love, and the energy of that love infuses everything I do with a feeling of wellbeing. Because of this, my creative flow becomes effortless, and everything I do brings me joy. When there is no inspiration, I resort to willing myself to be motivated. When I don't enjoy the process, the resulting artworks lack any emotional power. Among my friends, there are several professional artists who are economically motivated, but they are not artistically inspired. They create painting after painting, living by their motivation and wondering why they are not happy with the process.

What they don't realize is that being motivated is forcing them to live up to the idea of being a successful artist, which means competing with other artists, and holding them up as a measurement to judge what they are doing. When we try to use our will to motivate us towards a goal, we lose our joy, and it leaves us with a feeling of emptiness.

One of the ways to separate inspiration from motivation is to be aware that at every moment we have a choice about how we live. As we become aware, we observe how those choices affect us. If we allow inspiration to be our guide, then each day can invite a new and exciting opportunity. When we feel the heart engaging in what is happening to us, we know that we are connected with a hidden source of joy!

POWER OF MUSE

In your light, I learn how to love;

in your beauty, how to make poems.

You dance inside my chest

where no-one else sees you,

but sometimes I do,

and that sight becomes this art.

RUMI

WHEN THE SPARK OF INSPIRATION brightens up our vision in some way, it moves us to find expression for it. Inspiration most often comes with a compelling desire to share, or to make a connection with the source out of which it evolved. We are empowered to move toward it, to act on it, or to seek the beauty that in some way brought this new light into our awareness. When inspired, we are energized to share the wonder that has allowed us to see and experience something in a new way.

The desire to connect with the source of our inspiration can lead us to create something extraordinary, discover a cure for a disease, solve a problem, find a new land, go to battle for something we believe in, or to achieve a goal of some kind. Once inspired, something opens up within us and we are prompted to embrace the unknown to bring a new richness and possibilities to our lives.

This prompting is a driving power that guides us to birth a new reality. A portal of possibility opens and something deep within compels us towards new creative paths. My favorite word for this impulse is 'the friend,' because it is an empowering companion that befriends us. Artists have long described it as 'the muse,' because it is the personification of a playful imagination.

The muse can arrive as an inspiration, a seduction, a playmate, a dear friend, a mythical creature, but however it comes, it is a presence that beckons to us in a way that dares us to have fun and to live more joyfully. It awakens us at night, interrupts us when we are acting self-important, teases us to try something new and different, and helps us remember the excitement of being young and free and filled with hope.

The muse is a symbol of creative power, and it never fails to amuse us, to tickle our hearts, or to encourage us to remember how to play. It looks out for us, never leaves us, and it appears when we least expect it. We can try and silence it in any number of ways. We can refuse to listen, because we are afraid it will get us in trouble. There are so many voices in our lives telling us what we should be doing. This troublemaker may be the best friend we will ever have.

The call of the muse arises out of a feminine energy, while the masculine energy often comes through as a more assertive voice or through the flashing insights of a visionary. We would have a hard time following the development of the muse in history books, because we tend to fill our books with discoveries which have a more scientific basis. The muse has her own history in myth, legend and poetry, but as we can't prove its existence, we do not take it seriously enough. We feel safer with the reality of the outer world of results, than we do with what might have inspired them.

Although the surface description of the muse is elusive, it harbors a concept that is a stimulus for the creative process. Muse is something akin to the spirit, which connects our body with the soul. Perhaps the reason we have not taken this seriously in our culture is that we have not developed a consistent awareness of the integral connection between the soul and the body. The spirit is an activating and transparent agent of exchange between them. Labeling it supernatural or religious does not help to give it credence, because it steals the power from the heart and tries to bring it under the control of something or someone outside of us.

In the presence of the muse, creative energy awakens and acts as a catalyst to move the body, mind, heart, soul and spirit to flow together to craft a response. The moment I stand in front of a blank canvas with a paintbrush in my hand, I hear a clear message saying, *"It is the time to listen to the muse."* This voice is the spark that ignites the creative process of renewal in me. The Sufis refer to *khedr* as an experience with this presence that guides us to the creative wellspring of life and empowers us to give it physical expression. According to Sufis, *khedr* is the secret guide that whispered in the ear of Moses, giving his the path he had to take across Sinai desert. *Khedr* can appear to any of us at the moment of need. In Greek mythology, the muse is portrayed as the goddess of wisdom, Sophia.

Our muse is the voice from within that speaks a language we cannot comprehend on a literal level. It moves us through the waves of feeling that arise within our hearts. The symbolic forms and figures can frighten us, when it feels like they are leading us towards something that is unfamiliar to us. If we don't do it, because we are afraid, we will surely regret it. If we trust it and risk following the call of the muse, we have a certain protection within the movement of that action, because the muse does not guide us in a way that is wrong for us. We are accessing a deeper wisdom that is the wellspring of creative power. This is the source of great joy.

The muse conveys a guidance that excites us. The brain can bother and nag us with doubts, fears, and warnings. The rational mind can send a chill through us that causes us to question the simplest task and we become afraid. When the muse comes, we can dance on the rooftop in safety, as a deeper and more loving energy emerges and becomes a surrounding influence. We can come to know it as an empowering and watchful partner.

There is a story of a man who fell off a cliff while visiting the Grand Canyon, but halfway to the bottom of the valley below, he got caught on the branch of a tree. He hangs to the tree and screams, *"Help! O God help me!"* At that moment, he hears a voice from inside telling him to let go of the branch. He looks below and sees a drop of nearly five-hundred feet. He becomes frightened and screams for help again. The same voice tells him again to let go of the branch. Frightened and too full of doubt to follow his muse, he screams out loud, *"Is there another God out there?"*

When we feel the muse telling us to try something unusual or outside the routine we tend to follow every day, we become doubtful about following it. Following the muse opens a portal to a different dimension, and it requires a leap of faith to trust it. When we face an obstacle or come up against a limitation, our fear and apprehension can cause us to lose the clarity of our vision. Without the clarity of vision, the muse becomes confused, and we do not receive clear guidance. The more we trust, the more we let go of fear, the more familiar the process becomes, and we learn to welcome the presence of the beloved muse when it comes to us.

In my own life, the muse has been the power that guided me in taking steps beyond the acceptable standard in just about everything I do. I have grown used to learning new concepts in order to bring them into my conscious awareness. It is only through enhanced perception that we are free to transcend the limitations that confine us. The truth touches me in a creative way, and I am energized to take it to a new level that I have not experienced before. It moves me to face the unknown. I am fortunate that I took so many risks and followed them early in life. I didn't turn away, because giving up was not something I knew how to do. It was not in my nature, because I was encouraged to follow my muse all of my life. I am most grateful for that.

At the age of thirteen, I was selected to participate in a national painting competition for students. This took place in a camp located to the north of Iran next to the Caspian Sea. The assignment for the competition was to paint the landscape, looking out at a mountain across from the sea, covered with evergreen trees. My painting was almost done, when I noticed I still had more time, so I kept on using new colors on the painting to give it more energy.

As I was cleaning up the fuzzy parts of the painting, I suddenly noticed two riders appearing among the trees on the canvas. I had not had any intention of creating them.

The assignment was to paint the mountain, but something inside wanted to keep the riders, which looked more like two ghosts riding in the forest. Without touching the figures, I eliminated whatever was covering or blocking that image from being seen and handed the painting to the examiners. I was almost sure that my entry was going to be thrown out of the competition for non-compliance with the assignment.

The next day the winners were announced, and I saw the image of my painting on the front page of the newspaper as the first prize winner. The winning factor, as it was announced, was my ability to combine reality with fantasy. This had set my painting apart from others.

Through that experience, I discovered a power inside me, which guides me to paint what I am not able to by using my rational mind. I knew for a fact, that even if there were riders posing for me, I could not have painted what appeared on the canvas that day. From that time on, one of my excitements has been the discovery of the figures that appear on my canvas without any planning or intention of my own. I have learned that if I touch them directly, they are often ruined, so I usually draw them out by eliminating the extras around and in front of the 'self-appearing' forms.

Winning that competition opened a portal that allowed me to study European art. The prize was a three-month summer tour of European cities, where for the first time, I was able to stand in front of a Rembrandt, a Monet, or a Da Vinci masterpiece and experience the energy of the originals as my heart opened to those with vision. It was an opportunity to surrender to the flow of my own creativity and to broaden my perspective by learning from other creative people.

After that summer, whenever I started a painting, I would follow a certain approach, and if it did not feel it was the right way to go, I saw it as being at a crossroad where I had to choose a different way. Usually, one crossroad leads to another, and we follow the curves and the bends in the road. Sometimes, we cannot see where we are going, or where we are seems unfamiliar, but even though it is very challenging terrain, we keep going. Once we start questioning everything, we can lose our way.

In general, our life experiences help to develop our nature. At a certain point, when it becomes our nature to live creatively, we can feel when we are becoming aligned with our muse. From then on, we become like an oak tree that develops acorns, for it is the nature of the tree to do that. As we develop and discover our own given nature, we blossom as we were meant to. The muse is the centering influence that moves us to experience this joy and variation.

The guidance of the muse can easily be felt in a work of art, even though it is not seen with the outer eyes. The viewer makes a connection with their own muse, and they recognize and feel it within themselves. It is life's greatest gift to awaken to the rhythm and flow of what moves us from within. We learn to surrender and trust it, and we become excited to follow it. We are not seeking an end result. We are remembering how to play. If we try to control what happens, we are thrown off the playground. Children naturally follow the muse, unless they are taught otherwise. We feel the rushing stream of feelings breaking free, and we fall into the flow of the life-giving energy of love.

When I am standing in front of a canvas, I make choice after choice as I paint. If I lose the ability to make those choices, I am turning away from my own inner guidance. I compare what I am doing with what others have done, evaluating and thinking how people would react to it. When my creative power becomes my muse, I am placed in the arms of the beloved, the dance of love begins, and there is no more thinking. The beauty of the experience appears on the canvas because love guides the encounter with the source.

> *The boys were amazed that I could make such a poem as that out of my own head, and so was I, of course, it being as much a surprise to me as it could be to anybody, for I did not know that it was in me. If any had asked me a single day before if it was in me, I should have told them frankly no, it was not. That is the way with us; we may go on half of our life not knowing such a thing is in us, when in reality it was there all the time, and all we needed was something to turn up that would call for it.*
>
> MARK TWAIN

When we are touched by a deeper dream, we learn to follow a secret joy. The lover is someone with a secret. By listening to our hearts, we find our muse and we integrate the vision into our lives.

Creative people allow their lives to be centered in the heart. They become dedicated to the mysterious art of life, rather than being committed to poetry or music or painting or sculpture. The heart is the medium through which we express the vision. We begin by surrendering to the beauty of what transforms us. Mozart surrendered into a life of listening and following the music, and he became a course of creativity that is still flowing. We become an artist of life when we keep a vigil for the muse.

There is a deeply feminine dimension and a wonderfully masculine dimension present in the energy of creation, and their delicacy and majesty come together in a magnificent expression of beauty. Most of us feel separated from an awareness of our inner reality, and we can also be disconnected from our outer identity. It is because we haven't been attentive to the connection between the two. The muse helps us to fuse the two, to bring us into wholeness and give expression to our creative power.

We need to work on more clearly identifying the muse and exploring its spiritual connection as a source of our creativity. The muse deals with our feelings, our dreams, and our life experiences. Our dreams are inspired by what happens to us and how we integrate those events into our lives. Why should we ignore our own valuable experience and trust others to tell us what we should be doing?

When we follow our muse we are tapping into the source of our power for the development of our internal wellbeing. This is not the same as doing something for our physical welfare that deals with the rational mind. Following the muse involves acting on a faith that is guided by an entirely different pattern of energy. We cannot interrupt the flow when we are empowered by the muse. When we are following our muse and doing something for our internal development, we cannot suddenly stop in the middle of this creative process and try to think our way through it. It is risky to interject rational thought into the throes of the creative process.

The reverse is also true. When we are crossing the street, for instance, we are being rational in our observations and behavior as we follow the physical signs and the instructions we have been given. We cannot suddenly stop in the middle of this physical act and decide to do what we feel like doing. It becomes extremely dangerous.

Let us be very careful to identify the times to follow thought and the times to lose ourselves to feelings. This is discernment, and it is the challenge before us as we engage in the creative process of life itself. When we are immersed in the flow of the process, we must surrender to it, and we must stay surrendered. This is not for those who are faint of heart. This is awakening to a power that already exists, a process that is already in motion, inherent in the act of creation.

A soldier in a combat zone with instructions from his commanding officer would have a major problem if he decided to follow a different course in the midst of the battle. It could mean death, not only to him, but to those around him. It could also mean a court martial for not following the one in command. In some ways, following the muse is similar to a soldier following his superior's instructions.

In Taoism, Chinese Buddhism and Confucianism, the object is to become one with the Tao. When you follow the master, you follow everything the master says, for there is no such thing as being a partial follower. What comes to you through the heart, you do without questioning it. It becomes a problem if you shift the energy in the middle of the flow, whether you are following the muse in your internal development or if you are following instructions related to your external development.

If we want to develop our wealth, we need to realize our true wealth is in the treasure of who we are, who we are becoming, and how we integrate what happens to us into our expression. This kind of wealth is not just about the saving and spending of our money, it is what we accumulate in terms of the value of our life experience.

What is the fullness of our dream? What would be our maximum pleasure? It is the development of the creative power within us that brings this grace. Without it, we would be frozen before we ever came to life. The muse awakens the dream within our body and the power within our soul. It is the beautiful possibility of union that we are missing in our societal relationships, and it is the creative power we are missing in our political relationships.

To connect with our muse, we need to allow the creative presence to express itself within us, and let it transcend all the boundaries and limitations that exist around it. We awaken to become more aware of our deeper power, and eliminate all that would keep us from following its guidance. Step by step, with practice, we allow the muse to develop and expand us to bring our visions to completion.

It is possible for everyone to have a creative life. All we have to do is to make sure our outer and inner lives are companions on the path and are both open to the guidance of love. One cannot be a rival to the other. The flow of creative energy helps to find a balance in every aspect of life. A vision is formed in our heart and the muse guides it to expression. If we are creating from our own truth, and if we love what we are doing, the universe will help us find our way.

The muse awakens the dream within us. Artists have the courage to declare themselves artists, and mystics have the madness to declare themselves lovers. When we do this, we are already expanding in the direction of our intention. We are given clues to follow. We are fashioned after spiritual joy, a deep and profound pleasure of the soul that touches both our humanity and our divinity. When we feel the love that connects our hearts and souls and minds and bodies, we experience a union with the source of all creativity, and we learn to trust our muse.

POWER OF DISCOVERY

Lovers plant seeds wherever they go.

Love plants seeds wherever they fall.

Let the eyes of your heart open your vision

to vast unknown worlds.

RUMI

TO CREATE IS TO CONNECT with the power that manifests and moves the universe. As we play freely in the fields of creativity, we discover clues that lead us to make that connection. The muse is the power that sets the creative process in motion by perceiving the clues as inspiration.

The clues are always there, whether or not they are discovered is determined by the attitude of the person. There are times when the process starts with a very positive attitude, but when there are no immediate results, the initial enthusiasm fades. Success is inevitable to those who do not lose their confidence and keep a positive approach along the way.

I often make a mess of forms and colors on the canvas as I am painting. Knowing that I have the capability to get myself out of this mess usually brings with it a willingness to continue on with the same positive attitude and willpower with which I started.

Mystical poets refer to holding the tip of the hair of the beloved and never letting go of it. The hair is a metaphor for the path to the beloved that leads the lover to the nearness and inspiration of the purest love. The curls of the beloved's hair refer to the winding, ups and downs that one has to face on the journey. The beloved is the ultimate personification of the mystery of love. The mystic is forever on a journey of spiraling experience with the expanding beloved. It is a thrilling path to the eternal. When the soft essence of love rises within the lover, the heart is awakened to the deeper meaning of how empowering it can be. Preserving the mystery keeps the seeker from diminishing or limiting the possibilities.

There are highs and lows that one has to experience on the way to success. The secret is accepting the process without imposing judgment on what happens. Longing is the deepest kind of love that instills the seeker with enough faith in the potential to continue the journey. The spiraling journey of creativity can become frustrating, and this is when we most need a centering influence to help us discover the guiding clues. As we surrender to the flow, the loving breath of the beloved draws us to open the eyes of the heart to discover the next clue.

When intention is clear, clues that lead to solutions are recognizable. The clues lie in what attracts us in the deepest way. No matter where we are in the journey, the muse is the navigator that reaches out and points the way. It works like a breeze bringing a fragrance of sweet remembrance that turns our heads to its source. Sometimes, we may trip and fall and find ourselves in the mud, but when we trust the muse, we somehow manage to discover the clue that gets us back on course.

The ability to see a guiding light usually develops in the midst of darkness. We don't walk around in the sunlight using a flashlight to light the way. Yet in the dark, the light of our longing is like a lighthouse sending out a beam to guide us. Many of those who have discovered the way to their highest expression tell us that they found their own creative path during the darkest times of their journey.

If we have not allowed ourselves to envision our hopes and dreams in any way, or we do not feel the longing for something more, we will not be able to discover the clues to realizing creative living. The absence of intention can leave us randomly drifting in the shifting winds without any clear direction.

During my college years, two other students and I ventured into the forest to paint. We wandered deep into the forest, searching for a spot that provided a good view of the trees and then we painted all day until the sun was disappearing over the horizon. Two of us finished our paintings, and were preparing to leave, but our other friend was still painting. As darkness approached, the two of us who had finished became worried about being in the forest at night, afraid that we might lose our way in the dark.

Our friend, who was still painting, was quite relaxed and continued without paying any attention to our concerns. When we told him that we were going to leave him and go, he laughed and told us we would not find the way without him. We decided to stay and wait for him to finish, for we knew he had been in the forest before and seemed confident that he knew which way we had come.

Finally, he finished his painting, but the forest was getting quite dark by then. The two of us who had been waiting started to run, eager to find our way out before it grew any darker. Our friend was just walking along like he was enjoying the scenery. We were nervous and afraid, and we did not know why he was so calm until he finally showed us the reason for his composure. There were three round rocks laid on top of each other next to a tree on the floor of the forest. On the top one, a small white arrow was painted that was pointing a certain direction. Under it, on the second rock, the number 1.5 was written, which meant 1.5 miles to the edge of the forest.

Earlier, when we were walking into the forest, the two of us were not looking for the guiding clues, while our friend was paying attention and closely following them. There were three rocks, one on top of the other, placed every hundred yards and these clues would help us to find our way through the forest. We relaxed, and the rest of the walk was much more enjoyable for us. All the time we were panicking that we might lose our way, we were surrounded by the guidance of clues that were there to help us – if we had only been open and aware enough to discover them.

Sometimes, finding clues is so simple that it almost seems ridiculously easy. When we are inspired, in the confidence that we are guided by the creative energy of those who have gone before us, we feel the surrounding influence of a 'presence' that actually seeks our wellbeing. If we are passive and only learn to react, we become the victims of circumstance. The sooner we evolve toward becoming a creator of our own lives, the sooner we discover the guiding clues. As we relax and trust, the universe feels more welcoming, even friendly. This makes a great deal of difference when it comes to feeling aligned with the energy of creation. In effect, we trust our own hearts to look out for us. Perhaps this is the very transformation that led the mystics to call the beloved, 'the friend.'

Clues are usually discovered when there is a continuing sequence that leads from one to the next. Finding the clues involves an approach that is similar to the stepping stones in the fog that we discussed in the chapter on visualization, where one clue opens the way to discovering the next one. Persistence is the attribute that helps us to be more creative as we continue our journey. As we confront each challenge along the way, we learn something new which helps us to become more comfortable with what is unknown to us.

A major reason that people fail to complete the journey and realize their dream is that they lose the drive to even search for the clues at some point along the way. Something happens, they become distracted, and it pulls them away from their quest before they reach their goal. It is not surprising that they fall into confusion and lose their focus and direction in life, because they no longer have the attraction or longing that guides their muse.

If a person loses his focus during the process of creating, he can easily turn away from the path, because he would no longer be attending to the guidance of his muse. Where the focus is placed, plays an important part in determining the source of attraction and how to get there. If other events become distracting, or someone becomes overly concerned about what others are doing or saying or thinking or feeling, they can easily get lost in other people's business and lose track of their own. The persistence to follow one's own unfolding path declares the intention that keeps things in motion.

Being in the company of successful people or following in their footsteps is extremely valuable, especially at the beginning of the journey when one does not quite know how to discover the guiding clues. To keep the company of those guided by great aspirations is like finding a shortcut along the path. Learning about the life of those who radiate the energy of creative living, or reading their words, can be vital for completing the journey of creativity, because success leaves some very visible clues.

A guide is needed; don't journey alone! Don't enter the ocean blinded by pride.
Guidance is necessary to find your path. A guide is a shelter in your search.
Since you can't discern a cliff from a bend in the road,
how can you cross without a cane?
The road is long, and you are blind. Your guide keeps watch over the way.

ATTAR

Regardless of what path is being followed, clues are usually discovered through those whose awareness truly arises from within the heart – the ones who have tapped into an infinite source of a guiding light. Discovering the path does not necessarily require a recognized sage or a master as a guide. Guidance can come from those who are connected with a higher wisdom through their own hearts.

One year, my wife and I decided to take our children on a trip to Jamaica to participate in a Sunsplash Reggae Festival. When we arrived at the Montego Bay airport, we were told that our suitcase was missing. My wife was upset that all our clothing was lost, and I was frustrated over why she had to bring such a full suitcase of things to wear since we were only there for a few days of vacation on an island.

Disappointed and frustrated, we got into a taxi to go to our hotel. On the way, I started a conversation with the driver by asking him if he had a large family. He answered, *"No sir! I like to travel light!"* That simple statement, considering the condition we were in, was one of the most valuable clues and lessons that I received from anyone in my life. During those few days in Jamaica I decided to unload whatever was not absolutely necessary in my life. There is no question that this decision strengthened my resolve to follow and live in the power of creativity in a way that was right for my own life.

When on a creative journey, carrying too much of what is not absolutely needed becomes a major factor in deciding which direction to take. Finding the way, often means a person needs to be enthusiastic and utterly bewildered enough to freely discover clues in a way they might not otherwise perceive. When attention is paid to the muse, to insights and intuition, to whatever is attracting us, the path will open in a mysterious way. Excessive possessions that could slow down the journey need to be reduced to free up attention and allow focused observation.

When clues are directly followed, the companionship of the muse or 'the friend' continues to develop certain behaviors that are unique inspirations to each person. To inspire means to go inward and discover the spirit. It is to turn inward and melt, dissolve and fall into the beauty of the spirit of love. It is experiencing a fusion of the body with the soul. Whatever happens, it becomes an asset to help facilitate the flow of creativity.

When a creator becomes one with his creation, what he creates returns the beauty of the intention to him, very much like what happens to lovers when making love. To create, we need to feel as if the creation already exists in the mystery, and we are setting out to discover it, coaxing and inviting it to reveal its inner beauty to us. David was already in the marble when Michelangelo chipped away all that was not David to discover the perfection of form. We know it is invisibly present in creation, and we seek and pursue the revelation of its hidden face. We follow the clues to the source of love, and when it appears, we greet it with wonder, surprise, and excitement, and receive it with humility and gratitude. There is a deep pleasure in this kind of gift that allows us to feel the harmony between creator and creation. The harmony is a peaceful anointing of our existence. Goethe said:

> *Whatever you can do or dream, you can begin it.*
> *Boldness has genius, power, and magic in it.*

During my creativity retreats, I don't try to guide people to live my way of life, but I do encourage everyone to be in touch with their own dreams and to manifest them in the ways they are given to do that. Our truth is never about imitating another. If we allow and support others to find their own clues, we help them to become creators of their own existence, in their own style and with their own way of doing it. Everyone's own life experiences become signs and clues that help them find their direction.

In guiding people to create, I make them feel whatever they are doing is right in their creative work, constantly reminding them about the existence of their own brilliant light. Everyone is capable of being unique. I mirror their creative power and reflect their attractiveness to them. It acts as a summons for their own inner power to appear and come to their assistance.

When a person believes in their ability to express their own feelings, they are able to offer something worth giving and sharing to others. If an artist becomes blocked, and feels unable to open the flow creatively, they need to reach deeper for what they are holding back within themselves, for they can do better than they actually think they can. It is through building an expectation and a confidence in one's personal value that greatness can emerge.

When we are free and in touch with our deeper nature, life becomes a series of encounters of making and creating love. We focus on the beauty of that experience. When we feel and truly experience it, the immediate and natural response to it is to want to arouse love in the hearts of others. We want to help develop it in others in any way we can. This is when the law of attraction comes into play. This is how our dreams and thoughts are transformed to become an attractive energy to help guide others.

POWER OF DESIRE

Desire is the starting point of all achievement, not a hope, not a wish, but a keen pulsating desire which transcends everything.

NAPOLEON HILL

DESIRE IS A SECRET POWER THAT our bodies hold to attract what we are seeking. It is the glue that connects body and soul together. It is the originator of all creations and the alchemy that transforms dreams into reality. When we imagine something in our dreams, we desire it so much that our mind becomes convinced that we already have it and that places us in the flow of creativity. When we utilize the power of desire without resistance, we become a conscious creator who is fully empowered to manifest our dreams.

The fire of desire is the catalyst for the creation of every great work of art, every delicious meal that is cooked with love, every discovery, and every bridge connecting two lands together. Every action, whether it is viewed as good or bad by others, is prompted by the desire to become the inspiration that moves the world. Desire is the natural longing to obtain or possess that which brings us feelings of joy and satisfaction, and prompts a surrendering union to realize oneness with the empowering attraction.

I believe that human beings are placed here on Earth to express and create new things. Within every heart, the grace of love is seeking pathways that allow the creative process to flow as a natural expression. Desire prompts the heart to surrender into the process that allows this to happen, as the muse prods, stimulates, attracts, and arouses the discovery of the true feelings that lie beneath the protections we have constructed.

Desire moves us toward the flow of energy as it dissolves our reticence to surrender. It expands and blossoms in a way that is unique to each person. Without even knowing it in a conscious way, a divine energy is activated by desire, like an angelic impulse to spread the wings of freedom. The inner child is always longing to play, laugh, imagine and express the beauty of innocence by creating new worlds in the universal sandbox.

This marvelous divine energy co-exists with the compromising human side of trying to please others. The muse spins new dreams, prompting us to listen to the voice of love that issues forth from the heart.

The power of this driving force is the deep yearning, called desire! Creating a connection with the longing for caressing touch is much like longing for the beloved. Without this desire, we lose the momentum to be able to begin the day in a way that fuels and moves life forward into the hopes and dreams that have been hidden in the heart.

The very word, desire, comes from a Latin word, *desidere*, which means *from the star*. This suggests desire is the divine longing for the unknown, or a deep wish to know the secrets of the mysterious, symbolic light of the stars. Desire flows from the heavens, and to follow this pulsing guide is to create and follow 'our own special star,' the way so many others have done in many stories. It is a marker to indicate something new is about to happen. The light of desire vanishes behind the clouds and then appears again even more dazzling than before, reflecting a glow of divine radiance.

The longing suggests that something is absent, and there is an inner desire to go searching for what is missing. The heart yearns for the mysterious source of the light within all life. Desire is the guide for unity and oneness when we feel the lack of the intimacy of love. D. H. Lawrence wrote, *"Men are not free when they are doing just what they like to do. They are free only when they are doing what the deeper self truly desires. And to reach within to realize the nature of that self, takes some deep diving."*

Desire arises from the feeling of being away from the source of creative power. It becomes a powerful magnetic attraction to return home to the source of that energy and to discover it in the human heart. Sufis identify the earthly beloved as a 'loving friend,' and the divine beloved as 'the Friend,' which is an endearing name for the highest and divine love of God. The two are drawn together in the energy of longing, the vibration that closes the separation through union. When the archer draws back the string of a bow, and releases the arrow toward the mark, the flight of the arrow unites with the intention and direction of the one aiming the bow. Love fuses with and guides the flight and movement of the arrow, for love is also the target and all becomes one through the act of union.

Desire is the driving power that moves humanity toward fulfillment. Without it, goals are difficult to reach. When we examine the life of people who have reached a level of success in meeting their goals, we realize how overwhelming desire brings personal energy to the process. Most have faced their challenges by moving through the barriers toward the deeper intention of their goals.

Mike Tyson, onetime heavyweight champion of the world, followed his desire to fight in order to be wealthy and to make sure his family was financially secure. After he lost his final fight, he said, *"I lost my desire, I'm not hungry enough anymore. I'm wealthy; my kids have money, and I have nothing more to fight for."* Since he had the money, fulfilling his ego to be the champion didn't matter to him anymore. He no longer had any real desire to fight. His thoughts and feelings were not energized in the same way as an appliance is not ignited when electricity does not flow through to it from the source. The energy of desire was not aligned with his goal to bring the focus necessary to empower his drive to win.

A longing or attraction that forms from a deep desire can be a greater power than simply being determined to make something happen. Having a strong desire is to be compelled to take action by doing something to manifest a personal intention, and the key to it depends on the ability to hold focus on whatever it is that desire seeks to create. It can also depend upon the amount of energy that is put into action in manifesting our intention.

Ever since I can remember, I have had a burning desire to live in America. While going through high school, I watched every American movie that I could and studied the works of American artists, especially Norman Rockwell, to learn more about life in America. *Desidere* is perhaps a true description of how I was feeling. America was like a guiding star to me, I felt connected with it, and yet I was very far away from it.

To travel to America, I needed a passport and a visa. The passport was not too difficult to obtain, but getting a visa at my age was quite challenging. I had to have someone in the United States who could be responsible for my life while I was there. I went to the US Consulate General to discuss my dilemma with someone and ask for guidance. As I walked in, I noticed a picture of John F. Kennedy in the entrance hall of the building. It was a black and white photograph, which to me was not very complimentary and did not do him justice, so I decided to paint a portrait of him. I gathered as many photos of him as I could, and painted a life-size color portrait of Kennedy, had it framed and offered it as a gift to the consulate general's office.

The staff of the Consulate General could not believe a young person had done the portrait. They were very appreciative and replaced the black and white picture with this new portrait. I was thrilled. My painting was hanging on the wall of the American Consulate General's office. This was beyond anyone's expectation, even mine. Two months later, I had a passport and a visa to visit the United States. I was on my way to fulfilling my desire, which eventually led to my being granted US citizenship.

A deeply held desire is similar to a star that becomes the guiding light for the muse. It may disappear for a while behind the clouds of the challenges that one faces in life, but when the skies clear, it appears again and the light is familiar. When I found that getting a visa to come to America was not as easy as I thought, my personal sky clouded over, and I lost sight of the star of my desire. It was the shining light of hope and my personal desire that guided me to find ways to overcome my difficulties.

I moved post-haste in pursuit of my heart's desire. There was much I didn't know, like the English language or where I would stay when I arrived. I ran full speed ahead, right up to the edge of the cliff of all that was unknown, clinging to my intention to help me make that giant leap toward the life and career I wanted. I took the risk and let my desire lead me.

Like the three wise men, whose desire became the navigator on the journey to reach the birthplace of baby Jesus, I watched for the clues and tried to stay aware of what would help me reach my goal. Whoever is following a star of desire has to constantly check the clues to discern and verify that the muse is moving them toward the fulfillment of their dream and to reach the guiding star. Purity of heart ensures that the desire is aligned with the dream. There are always obstacles and gathering clouds that obscure the view on the way, but by truly following the heart's desire, grace lights the path, and the universe responds and supports the journey. Without having any idea how it will happen, we follow the star through faith.

The positive energy of creativity fully engages a person in a deeper desire. The ultimate source of desire is the soul's impulse to express itself in the world. This is not something that goes away or just disappears on its own. A person's physical being harbors the energy within, and hopefully, the heart learns to recognize it. When the creative power is blocked in some way, the desire is easily lost, and so are the guiding clues.

The creative process helps us to investigate, to shape, to redirect, and to delight in the flow of desire. When this happens, taking a risk is like reaching for the joy of creating. We feel a flash of energy, like lightning, that commands attention. Fulfilling that deep desire brings an inner peace and a sense of wellbeing. Being absorbed in the energy of desire produces a radiant glow – a very special aura. Finding a way to express the inner world through an outer expression is an energizing and life-giving process.

We need to be fully attentive to attraction, and especially to the desires that stir the heart. We have to honor them by acting on the guidance of the muse. Finding expression for desire is one of the greatest joys of life. Missing the opportunity to do this, could cause the loss of an inner vision that was realizing and manifesting creatively in some way.

Following the desires of the heart is creating without trying to control the process or having to know how it works. The heart can be moved to express a dream. Even though the eyes might be creatively blind, the heart can be moved by a deeper energy that moves within, already flowing and guiding in a way beyond the imagination. William Blake wrote:

> *Abstinence sows sand all over*
> *the ruddy limbs and through the flaming hair,*
> *but Desire that is gratified,*
> *plants fruits of life and beauty there.*

Although the energy of desire is an exceptionally creative urge, it is best to allow it to develop through conscious awareness. It is helpful to be aware of the motivating desire and the reasons for actions that affect personal behavior. There may not be judgment about the process, but it would help to discern more clearly by realizing what the possible consequences might be. When acting on a subconscious impulse, it is quite difficult to be aware of how this might affect others. Creativity can move the flow of life into the unknown very quickly, and although the mystery is appealing, the results can be overwhelming. Many unexpected surprises could happen when seeking to satisfy the desire to realize a dream. Being full of care will help to diminish the damaging effects of following desire without regard for anyone else.

When a person is lacking sufficient desire to be motivated to search or is feeling indifferent about making a journey, they need to discover what might truly activate the desires hidden within their heart that would move the creative spirit. Without arousal and the desire of attraction, there is little incentive to begin any creative process. Yet, the surprising appearance of strong desire can suddenly flood and infuse the entire being with a new energy!

Blessed by the source of this wonderful life-giving impulse, the heart can open to the creative flow that moves as freely as the energy of creation itself. A prayer of gratitude and remembrance is a divine recognition of the mysterious energy from which all life has been created.

POWER OF FAITH

On a long journey of human life,
faith is the best of companions;
it is the best refreshment on the journey;
and it is the greatest property.

BUDDHA

FAITH IS AN ASSURANCE THAT what a person hopes for will somehow in some unforeseen way happen! It is an invisible support that sustains and empowers us to embrace the unknown with confidence. Faith might not manifest as imagined, but can guide us to recognize the signs and energy that flows from the mysterious source that seeks our wellbeing.

One of the main reasons many people never draw on their creative capacity is that they have no faith in the marvelous energy available to them. They fall into becoming a consumer of what they can acquire rather than learning to create the life they truly want. It seems it is easier for a person to simply believe they are not creative enough than it is for them to dare to discover and develop the abilities that would help them achieve a meaningful life. There are people who inspire us to believe we can have the life we want, and there are those who convince us that we need their help to achieve our goals. Whether the choice is conscious or not, the direction we take is up to us.

Faith empowers the energy that guides everyone toward their ultimate capacity. It is the flashlight that shows the way toward what is going to be created. It is a powerful help in moving us forward. Faith is the architect that designs each life.

Faith has great potency in activating our creative power. It can achieve startling results and produce what many people call miracles. Faith is inherent in everyone, even when it works unconsciously and independently of the object on which it is focused. The cultivation of true faith is an absolutely necessary discipline in creativity. In fact, the creative process cannot even begin without it. We must have faith in the presence of the muse within our own hearts and have steadfast faith that we can seek and receive its guidance.

The gift of faith opens the possibilities in life and helps us to discover the interior vision that inspires creativity. There is a radiant light inside every heart that connects with the source to activate the faith to create. This is perceived rather than consciously known. Michelangelo spoke of it as *intelleto*, or the divine intellect, which is an important concept in understanding faith.

The nature of everyone and everything exists inside them. An artist of life learns to free the infused vision. When Michelangelo chipped away at the marble to free the statue of David, his hands were guided by his faith as he released the vision of perfect form that was placed within the stone by the divine intellect. Ironically, everyone has that perfect form concealed inside the outer image. When there is faith, it is easy to tap into the vision and learn how to clear the way for that inner beauty to reveal itself.

Anyone who pursues a dream or seeks to bring a vision into reality will sometimes encounter obstacles along the way. Where there is no faith that the journey can be carried through, people can react in more practical ways, by choosing solutions that fall short of their hopes and dreams. That is a way of becoming consumers of other people's creative abilities without realizing that the energy and ability to follow the heart's desire exists within everyone.

There are people who deny the powerful impact of faith and negate its manifestations. The fact is, what they call providential, intervention or coincidence can all be traced to faith, which is the true source. One of Albert Einstein's precocious students went to visit him. After the visit, they walked out onto the porch and the young man pointed to a tree, *"Dr. Einstein, how do we know the tree is there?"* Einstein replied, *"Only by faith!"*

Much of what is today considered unexplained has to do with occurrences of faith. Some define faith as ignorant superstition because they know very little about how faith works. They say that faith cannot make anything happen and consider, *"With faith all things are possible,"* to be a false statement. Yet, we have heard of physicians who have cured their patients from major pains by just giving them vitamin pills, making them believe they were pain relievers.

There are many examples of how faith develops a self-confidence that leads to success and how the lack of it may bring failure. Modern psychology gives us accounts of people with no physiological disability who were incapable of walking because they thought they had suffered a paralyzing injury to their legs.

The creative process does not move without faith. Buddhists call faith the 'seed' without which, spiritual development cannot take place. In Sanskrit, the word for faith is *shraddha*, which is similar to *cor*, meaning the heart, in Latin. We see in both of these ancient cultures that faith is more a quality of the heart than of the mind. Faith is the perception of the heart and transcends that of the intellect.

In the journey of Jesus, as told in the stories of his time, he tells people over and over that it is their faith that has saved them. When a woman who touched the hem of his robe is healed, Jesus assures her that it was her faith which healed her. The message that faith is a healer is repeated many times.

We often project the power to heal onto someone or believe an object has the power to bring about change. It is a mystery why some are healed, and others are not, but it is possible that a powerful faith can activate a cellular memory of wellness. Those who bring light to others, help them recognize the divine spark that dwells within them.

The strength of our heart's desire helps to activate faith and to expand our belief in the self so as we can achieve results beyond what we could otherwise envision or imagine. It opens a portal into a new world of possibilities and encourages us to make a leap of faith beyond what can be known or described. There are countless personal stories in every culture to prove this. Physicists call it the quantum leap, artists describe it as an imaginative idea, but no matter what it is called, it is an act of faith that causes a person to move toward solutions that are unknown and untested. The incredible gift of faith opens a closed mind, and suddenly, a light appears that shows a new way of perceiving. That is when one would appreciate what it means to be saved by a strong faith. It is often said that the sea did not part for Moses until he took the first step of faith into the water.

Those who have faith in unseen possibilities are more at peace with themselves than most. They are not subjected to all the mental questioning and anxiety that many experience. Their internal faith inspires them, so that no matter what comes around, they will find their way to a peaceful solution. Having doubt about your ability to find creative solutions will not improve a situation, and certainly, negative thinking does not make things happen.

Doubt causes a person to question whatever is happening or to become fearful of what may be ahead and forms the repetitive, circling pattern of a worried mind, but it will not find its way into the heart sustained by a strong faith. Doubt can only break through weakness. Through faith, everyone is able to become a co-creator of his or her own life.

There is a story of a traveler who wanted to cross the Mississippi in the early days of the west, but he could not find a bridge to cross. It was a cold winter and the great river was covered with ice. The traveler did not know how thick the ice was and was doubtful that he could walk across the frozen river, so he cautiously began creeping across on his hands and knees. Suddenly, he heard the sound of a carriage from behind. Before he could turn his face to see what was going on, another traveler passed by driving four-horses and a load of coal over the ice, singing a happy song!

To have faith is to accept the challenges and obstacles along the way as a natural part of life. This kind of faith is built through experience and the determination that nothing can take us off the path. We learn not to consider obstacles, distractions, or even pain in a negative way, and we come to recognize them as part of the process. Although it can be painful at the time, when we look back in reflection, we can see that an experience may have been necessary to get to where we are.

To develop faith, one needs to believe in the presence of an inner power that is our divine guide. We need to learn to trust that it is always with us and experience reveals the truth of this guidance. A gardener knows how to nurture and care for what he plants. He looks out for what he has planted in the garden. The source, out of which we come, provides for us in ways that our rational mind is incapable of recognizing. The leap of faith gives us access to creative power that already exists within us, grants us peace of mind, and it guides us to discover the ultimate reason for life itself. Mahatma Gandhi said, *"Faith can only grow from within, it cannot be acquired vicariously. Nothing great in this world was ever accomplished without a living faith."*

If it weren't for the faith of the few, the artistic development and technological advancement that we all enjoy today would have been impossible to achieve. Faith is the powerful energy that guides desire. Creativity is for those who do not indulge the fear of failure. They have learned to create in so many ways that they develop faith in discovering a creative result.

I do not claim a belief in a higher power that favors certain people over others, and I certainly don't think any higher power would so exclusive as to consider only a few of us as the chosen ones. The chosen are those that choose to embrace the promises, those who trust the gifts of faith, hope and love. The invitation is for everyone.

Faith is not the same as belief. Although they are interrelated, there is a subtle difference. Belief is a product of the mind, and is formed based on ideas and concepts that are gathered through information and experience. Belief is rooted in culture and upbringing, and can change over time as more knowledge and experience is gained. Changing the mind is changing some aspect of one's beliefs.

Faith is belief that is not based on proof. It can also be defined as having full confidence or trust in whatever comes along. When we believe with enough confidence to take action we exercise faith. Knowing does not create faith, unknowing does.

A believer opens their mind to the truth only when it corresponds with his preconceived ideas and wishes. One who is faithful opens their heart to the truth without reservations, and is prepared to accept whatever it may turn out to be. Faith is the essential virtue of creativity, not belief. When we develop faith in our capabilities, it frees us to create, streamlines our lives, and helps us to experience joy.

Recognizing the difference between faith and belief is essential in the creative process. There are times when we are in the middle of creating something when we need our faith and we run into crisis when we confuse it with belief. We try different approaches in the belief that one way should work, and another way will certainly not work, and we find out nothing fits or matches. Our beliefs, however deep, educated, flexible, magical or well-thought out, do not get us the result we are seeking, and we can become discouraged, doubtful, terrified, and even begin to hate what we are doing.

Next time you find yourself in such a condition, give up on attaching value to your beliefs, whether they are positive or negative. Give them up, just for the time being, and do not labor at bringing them into a situation because you think they will help you with your crisis. Free yourself of the destructive flow of self-doubt, of your belief in limitation, and your lack of awareness. Have faith that anything you do to resolve the problem will do just that, and witness how exciting the process becomes as you shed the light of faith on what you are creating.

Belief is like a dense cloud that smothers the spark of faith. We fall into error when we rely only on our own knowledge and thoughts. Train yourself to recognize when you become too anxious and want to hurry the result. When we act hastily – relying on our belief rather than having faith – we break our connection with the Source and ignore it. When we fall into this confusion, we deprive ourselves of this most precious gift of grace. Trust the guidance of your muse. Fall in love with the creative power that awakens you from sleep and sings an enchanting song beneath the moon. Learn how to listen and see with the eyes and ears of love. When we glimpse another in the light of perfect love, we will know and feel the power of faith. We recognize and remember this exhilarating energy, for it sparks a remembrance of empowering love when it surges through us.

To make full use of the power of faith, one needs to learn the art of surrender, to clear the way for the purity of truth and of love that is not self-seeking. We need to center in the beauty that gives itself for the pleasure of all, and we need to reconfirm our connection with the creative source. Our faith will not be diminished if we are always in relationship with the truth of who we truly are. Listen carefully and follow the guidance of your muse and above all, be grateful for connecting with the mystery of it that guides you to share in the creative process. Gratitude carries a positive energy that enhances and empowers faith.

Acting on faith and coming to know the muse, makes us realize that we are in the hands of the 'Gardener' and everything is unfolding and revealing itself at the perfect time. We will become aware of the help the universe is sending and the resources that are suddenly available to us. Relationships will come to us at the very moment we need them. When we don't know where to turn, what direction to take, or how we will ever realize our dream, our faith opens the door to a deeper vision.

The single most important act in this life is to have faith that love is alive within everyone. With this faith, we can surrender consciously and willingly to be a channel for the creative energy to find expression through us. As we do this, we experience the purity of love, and we fall into the creative flow. There is no greatness without humility, and no gift that expands without a grateful heart. We are loved. That love awakens us to the presence within and we willingly share in that transforming energy, in whatever ways we have been prepared to express it.

Names dissolve in the power of faith, and the beauty of essence pools in the streaming light that illuminates everything. Faith is magnified, multiplied, and embraces and surrounds all life in the expanding spiral of the spirit of love. It has an infused power that is stronger than anything else in the world. It has no opposite. It casts out all fear and all selfish desires that people may have had to keep anything for themselves alone.

To undertake any creative endeavor, we need to have full faith in its success. Whether we are writing, painting, acting or setting the dinner table, each is a creative act, and we need to take a leap of faith to achieve it. The secret of successful living rests on how we develop enough faith to feel assured that we are not making a mistake, nor being afraid of making one.

Whatever life brings, we are given faith so as we can live creatively if we truly seek to. Faith develops us, and it is faith that opens us to the source of immeasurable power. We turn to our muse to guide us and move us through life from moment to moment, as we become vessels to express the beauty of love in the world. Faith helps to transform us into the messengers for the Creator of All Life, so that we may shine with the light and love that it is our grace and fortune to receive and experience. We open to the guidance that creates a pathway for the continual flow of the energy and spirit of love that sustains our lives.

POWER OF SEX

Sex is one of the nine reasons for reincarnation...
The other eight are unimportant.

HENRY MILLER

THE UNIVERSE IS DEEMED TO be the arena where positive and negative powers unite with each other. The same union that exists throughout the universe occurs in every being including the human body. In reality, creation is a sexual process. It is the fusion of masculine and feminine energies. Reproductive activity is a form of creativity that is directed toward creating and sustaining life.

Sexuality is the gate to the palace of creativity. It is true that some may climb the wall or find other ways to get in, but most people enter the palace through the gate. There are many reasons why sex has such an influence on the creative process, but most importantly, creative power arises from feeling. Sexual expression provides one of the greatest sources of passionate feeling that human beings can experience.

Creativity and sexual activity complement each other. When they are mindfully kept in balance, one enhances the other. We engage in sexual activities for the purpose of creating offspring, and if it is not specifically for that purpose, we are still aware of the attraction and how it works in our bodies as a creative process.

Sexuality is a clear demonstration of how the process of creation works to perpetuate life. Togetherness and the aesthetic of erotic play are not only genetic drives but also opportunities for the expression of sensuality. It is normal and natural for men and women of all ages to have a wide range of sexual experiences.

Sexual sublimation, according to Sigmund Freud, is the attempt to transform sexual impulses or what he called sexual energy into creative energy. Freud believed that the greatest achievements in civilization were due to the effective sublimation of sexual and aggressive urges that are sourced in the id and then channeled by the ego. He held that sublimation is a way to avoid confrontation with the sexual urge.

Most expressions of love are essentially sexual in their nature. Of course, sexual energy is not limited to the physical act of sex alone. The energy of sex is sublimated as creative energy at any and every level of the universe. Jewish mysticism views sublimation of the animal soul as an essential task in life, where the goal is to transform animalistic and carnal cravings for physical pleasure into the holy desire to connect with God.

In all my years of guiding individuals in ways to access the power of creativity in their own lives, there has not been an instance where sexuality has not come up in some way as an issue that needs to be discussed. It is a natural aspect of who we are, and it is closely connected to how we express our creativity in a variety of different and surprising ways.

When I am asked questions such as, *"How long will it take for you to finish a painting?"* or *"When do you know a painting is finished?"* or *"What is it that stimulates the beginning of a painting?",* I usually respond by repeating the question back to them with slightly different wording: *"How long does it takes to complete love making?"* or *"How do you know when it is finished?"* or *"What is it that stimulates you to engage in sexual activity?"* My point is quickly made. They laugh and realize that creativity, like sex, is not something that follows a certain standard.

The urge to be involved in sexual activities is the most powerful of all human desires. It arouses strong emotions that help develop imagination, courage and determination, as well as the ability to be more creative, all at the same time. We regularly hear about the significant sexual energy of some of the famous and talented people in politics and sports.

The history of every nation reveals that many men who made great achievements, gathered great fortunes or gained outstanding recognition in their fields had a high sex drive, and were very often motivated by the sexual influence of women in some way. Many have risked their reputations, their careers, their crowns and titles, and their fortunes for their sexual desires. Sexual feeling is an overpowering energy which allows men to become a super power for action. It is the desire for life in various forms. To many, sexual expression is such an irresistible force that, at times, nothing seems to be able to contain it.

Lord Byron had to have sex every time he started to write, which is why he slept with hundreds of women, as well as few men, each year. Titian had secret affairs with his models, Raphael died of sexual exhaustion, Tolstoy made his bride read detailed accounts of his past sexual affairs on their wedding night and Vivaldi, a priest, wrote his *Four Seasons* while living sinfully with two sisters. Balzac believed that a *person would make better art and would be more productive through experiencing sexual activity*. He is considered as being one of the premier 'horn-dogs' of his age, often having relations with several women in the same day, then writing all night. No wonder Rodin has sculpted him with an erection under his robe!

The greatest motivating power for both men and women is found in their desire to please one another. When sexual desire is used properly, it can bring us into a creative state far beyond what we can even imagine. Men have strived in order to appear great in the eyes of women, and women have gone to great lengths to be charming and attractive to men. The nature of this attraction has been constant throughout human history, even though the means of pleasing each other continues to change.

If you remove the influence of women from the life of most men who have created amazing art, accumulated large fortunes, and attained great heights of power and fame, everything they have gained might well seem useless to them. It is an inherent desire in most men to find ways of pleasing women. This is a vulnerability that can give women the opportunity to use a man's desire to manipulate men to get what they want. Men can seem to have strength and willpower when dealing with other men in business and society, but they can also be easily tamed and manipulated by women they desire.

The control of sexual energy calls for the development of great willpower, but the reward of this discipline is worth the effort. The desire for sexual expression is instinctual and a most natural function. We would do well to become more comfortable with our genetic function. It should not be repressed or eliminated from our lives and may surface at inopportune times if we try to ignore it.

The power of sexual desire can easily be transformed into creative expression. There are many forms of expression that would enrich our bodies, minds, and spirits – and be healthy outlets for sexuality! Just imagine how great it might be if those who have used sex to be abusive could have transformed that sexual urge to motivate others, to develop values and faith, and to do something truly creative to benefit everyone instead of just satisfying their own basic drives.

A river may be contained by a dam or an obstruction, and the water controlled for a time, but eventually, it forces an outlet and breaks through. The same is true of the sex drive. It may be suppressed and controlled for a time, but its very nature causes it to seek some form of expression. If sexual desire is not satisfied in one way or another, it may seek another kind of outlet, such as we see in the aimless physical indulgence of promiscuity, known in slang terms as 'sleeping around' in order to make conquests and have control over others.

We are rarely considered great because we possess a powerful sex drive. The majority of people tend to lower their goals and misuse this power at the level of their lower natures. Simply having sexual energy as a human characteristic, does not guarantee us the creative ability to use it well. The energy needs to be transformed and redirected from the obvious desire for physical contact into some other form of desire and expression, which gives us a choice to use it in a variety of constructive ways.

The greatest means of channeling sexual energy has been to move it in the direction of romantic love. Through the centuries, romantic love has inspired countless composers, poets, painters, and sculptors to charm the object or person of their desire into union. The energy of our longing to be united with another arises out of the remembrance or revelation of our oneness with all life.

One university study revealed that professional artists and poets often experience sex with almost twice as many partners as other people. This study showed that the number of sexual partners actually increased as the creative output increased. What is created draws attention to its creator, which also can manifest in a way that makes them more sexually attractive to others.

The inference is that the more creative we are, the more partners we will attract. The reason, according to the researchers, is that creative people tend to be more uninhibited, more outgoing, and their interests are more diverse. As a whole they are fun to be with, even though many may be disorganized, less likely to be logical, and may act on impulse rather than sticking to a plan. Generally, creative people may be more passionate, playful and imaginative with partners.

> *The artist's experience lies so unbelievably close to the sexual, to its pain and its pleasure, that the two phenomena are really just different forms of one and the same longing and bliss.*
>
> RAINER MARIA RILKE

We create because we seek to give some formal expression to our inner experience. Certainly, the inner experience is not always joyful and positive, but we still wish to share our feelings with other human beings. Our developing nature as human beings can harbor feelings such as anger, rage, anxiety, confusion, and inappropriate primitive urges. It is possible to use these feelings constructively in some kind of creative work. The intensity can give a work its quality, its power, and express the sharp edge of overwhelming emotions as they affect us in ways that help make us more aware of our darker moods and instincts. For example, a novel about the feelings of a serial killer can offer an outlet to examine what drives our thoughts and actions in an imaginative story line.

The desire to be creative, no matter what medium or field we express it in, coexists with the basic primal urge to sexually unite with another. Most creative people would say their creative motivation and projects have been built around some of their greatest passions. These can be a clear extension of the sexual drive. Passion can affect our thinking and enlarge our view of the world. Ultimately, this can be helpful in promoting creative ideas and solutions in how we experience the world.

Loving and experiencing our oneness with all life is the ultimate mystery that we are blessed to share. This attraction is what lifts us into a higher dimension of experience that touches the divine nature, which seems to be infused and preserved in a divine spark that exists in every one of us. The basic sexual urge becomes a springboard, a rocket launch, a fountain, a fire, a celebration of love purified by the spreading wings of the soul and the freedom of spirit that develops through transformation and transcendence. Some call this mysterious creative power an attraction to the 'Beloved.' We are lifted into the beauty of the spiritual heart. The mystic cultivates a longing for the sublime, for divine love, expanding and reaching toward a level of existence beyond the physical urge to reproduce and beyond the rational mind, yet there is no question it is empowered by the miracle of regeneration.

One of the underlying motives of artistic creativity may be to attract sexual partners. A number of musicians I've met have admitted they started or joined existing bands, or they learned to play an instrument, not out of any particular musical inclination, but rather to attract sexual partners, and a true interest in music developped only later on. Some of the same motivation seems to have created an attraction for other forms of the arts as well. It seems that wanting and seeking favors from another human being even without getting what they originally wanted has been the true generator of creativity for many artists. They develop an ideal that inspires their creations, whatever the artistic medium might be.

The same way that a person learns to play the guitar and sing in order to attract others, staging an artistic production might flow from a person seeking a means of expression as well as simply looking for an audience. Many works of art might not even exist if it weren't for the sexual motivation to create something to gain the approval of others. Showing a painting that expresses the beauty of a woman may well arouse sexual desire in the viewer. It excites others and makes many women feel more beautiful and more open to give of themselves. Many artists delight in taking advantage of that opportunity.

Jeff Koons, one of most well-known contemporary American artists, was a Wall Street broker who took an erotic turn and created his *Made in Heaven* series, in which he explicitly depicted himself having sexual relations with his wife Cicciolina, an Italian porn-star. Justine Lai, another contemporary artist created a series called *Join or Die*, in which she painted herself having sex with every US President in history. Andy Warhol was clearly obsessed by sex. His art often drew heavily on his participation in the gay community.

Hieronymus Bosch, a fifteenth century Dutch artist, who lived in a very moralistic little town in the Netherlands, painted erotic fantasies that seemed to explode the imagination. In the central panel of *The Garden of Earthly Delights* he has painted an exaggerated fantasy of total sexual freedom of naked 'savages' living in the new world in a natural state where men and women cavort with giant strawberries, ride bareback and make love in bubbles.

The sexual urge to unite and reproduce is such a powerful drive that it seeks expression however possible, through whatever means is allowed in one's environment. It is necessary to find some constructive way to release the tension generated in the physical nature of life seeking itself. Our civilization depends upon our drawing on this impulse, finding the flow through such a powerful force that will help us to use it well. If we are constructive and creative, it has the potential to become an incredible source of joy.

Of course creative ability does not spring only from sexual drive. There are a variety of sources for this expression, but the sex drive is an extremely powerful energy. There have been many gifted individuals who were incredibly creative, who seemed to have little interest in sex. It is worth noting that if a person's libido is weak, it certainly does not mean that they will have less creative talent. It seems to find its expression in other ways.

Going after whatever inspires a young artist is the secret to developing creative power, and sex is truly a great source of inspiration and energy at that age. Many artists would confess that the only thing that appeals to them is whatever feels sexually attractive. The goal of every creative person is to access the state of mind that great artists, inventors, scientists, and thinkers have experienced. That requires the stimulation of sexual desire, one of the most powerful feelings known to us as human beings. This elevates the senses, including the mind, to a heightened state of awareness and sensitivity.

An important consideration regarding sexual arousal and how it influences creativity is the recognition that there is a biological and procreative function to sexuality. This is a familiar concept in the material world, and a balancing opposite to the spiritual world. Although the two are considered separate, we know that they are interconnected in a way that is not obvious to our rational mind. What we need to do is to develop the awareness of how to work creatively with our sexuality and come to understand what it represents, rather than being lost in desire and becoming obsessive.

We don't have to become sexual or even engage in a sexual act with another in order to have our sexuality enhance our creativity. We need to consciously be aware of its effect in order to be able to redirect our sexual passion and transform it. The more conscious we are, the more we can use our creative desire constructively to achieve a goal that will benefit others as well as ourselves.

The power of sexuality rests in how we use it and whether we act on the impulse or not. If we do act on it, what is the chance of having sex only to reproduce, or simply to satisfy our desire for union. Alternatively, we can learn to see it as a gift that empowers us to create physically, mentally, emotionally, and spiritually. When we choose to use our ability to reproduce with a partner we love and respect, the sexual instinct is expanded to an even fuller expression, and both feel a part of the creative process. Hopefully, we use all of the possibilities in an integrated and more conscious way as we evolve creatively, which can be an exalting spiraling journey!

Sexual activity in procreating is obvious and we are all aware that it grants us the power to reproduce, and we are programmed genetically to move toward this end to breed our species. How we use it and whether we do it creatively or destructively is at a higher and more complex level of our choices that affect our evolution.

The process of civilizing and developing a primal urge through socialization is the subject of many books and paintings. In the historical novel by Jean M. Auel, *The Clan of the Cave Bear*, we learn about times when men just leaped on women from behind, which was a primal instinct without any real awareness of intention, but involved just following an instinctual urge. How we use the sexual drive and energy is as diversified as we are.

What is our intention? Is it mutual?

There are people who practice celibacy in order to expand their love and use it compassionately in service to God, and there are others who have no control over their sexual desires. When it comes to creativity, it is difficult to place a value judgment on something so universal. Did madness take over Vincent Van Gogh because he chose to be celibate, or was it helpful in creating those magnificent canvases? We can only admit that different consequences lead to a variety of results. Our diversity is becoming greater all the time, and our consciousness is continually expanding our choices.

When it comes to creative living, the experience of joy can only be extended and granted in accordance with each individual and whatever their moral standard might permit. The gift should nurture what it means to be fully human. When we participate mutually with a partner to co-create and are able to give birth to a living human being, or to create a shared life through a loving union, and when our intention is mutually clear, we experience the most astounding, amazing, and humbling flow of creative energy. We are incredibly blessed if we are able to truly awaken to this gift of grace.

POWER OF LOVE

When love beckons to you, follow him,
though his ways are hard and steep.
And when his wings enfold you yield to him,
though the sword hidden among his pinions may wound you.
And when he speaks to you believe in him,
though his voice may shatter your dreams
as the north wind lays waste the garden.

KHALIL GIBRAN

LOVE IS AN INTOXICATING AND bewildering energy that opens the flow of creativity. It leads us into a deeper experience, away from the weariness of the mundane life, toward the freedom and wholeness of our creative expression. The feeling of love is the power that arises from our deepest evolutionary roots and urges us to create, to generate new life, to regenerate our species. This joyful feeling is the fountain of strength and creativity that is released when we are free from judgment and allow our limits to expand.

Love is a mysterious, ecstatic feeling that activates the inner life of an artist to create works that are uninhibited, and freely and skillfully expressed. It is the energy that draws a person into the deeper and more sacred areas of the psyche. When people tell me they love a certain work of mine, it brings me confidence, but when I personally love what I am doing, it makes me fearless. Writing, painting, composing, observing and playing, all require daring submission to the process of being swept into this ecstatic energy, toward a transformation of the self, in a similar way to what happens when we fall in love with someone.

Creativity comes in naming our own icon, in envisioning our own creative inspiration to make our own journey to awakening! This is the beauty of dreaming and the process of giving birth to it in some form in our own life. When the power of love is directing the creative process, there is no need for enhancing or beautifying what is being created. The ability to create, which can take years of practice and experience, can be expressed in one moment through the power of love. Thousands of skilled brush strokes cannot show what a single stroke that is led by love can express.

Love connects hearts through the creative process. When we create through pure love, we make a safe place for others to dream. We set them free to travel the valleys and peaks of transformation! As Huckleberry Finn finds his magic in the Mississippi River through Mark Twain, we dream with him as he explores the unknown. If Don Quixote fights his battles for his ideal woman, it is not ours to take away from the vision of Cervantes. If Beethoven creates a sonata inspired by his beloved, it is not our place to limit what he envisions.

Works of art are created for a variety of reasons, but above all else, every creation flows from a source of joy and love. We live for the joy of being, and out of that joy, the infinite expression of form and learning and compassionate activity evolves. When I love what I do, I know that I am expressing my love in the form of a painting. My imagination is the driving power behind it, and just like other lovers, I am not concerned about what others might say about it.

The consistent mysterious factor, that keeps the power of creation moving through every obstacle, is the inherent love of creating. Whether it is a child, an artwork, a way of life, invention, new forms of healing, sculpture, weaving, composition, playing music, singing, dancing, bringing laughter to people, there are thousands of ways we can invite and welcome others to feel joy through our creativity!

Love is the truth that brings eminence and raises our consciousness from the earthly plane to higher levels. The same way as the moon is prominent among the stars, lovers stand out shining among other people. It is only through love that we are able to experience the exalted life that we were meant to live. As we reach that level, the ordinary life begins to seem limited, confined and contained in a much smaller world. It is somewhat like the joy of playing in an unlimited free space as opposed to being contained within the boundaries of a prison cell. When we are released from confinement, we become immersed in creativity, like the sun pouring infinite rays of its radiance upon Earth. A creative person does not see the self, because it has been surrendered into the energy of love.

The same way that a flower blooms as it feels sunshine, a work of art flourishes through the love of its creator. When a creative work is evolved through love, what is invisible to the eyes becomes visible to the heart, because love comes flowing through it. Love can flow through anything, split it open, dissolve it, melt it, and make it bloom, or make the person so powerful that he is able to create what he could not even envision in his dreams.

One of the most powerful instances of how divine love cultivates the creative power is the love of Rumi for Shams and its eminent impact on his life. Prior to meeting Shams, Rumi, who lived during the twelfth century, was a Moslem cleric, a leader and a spiritual guide to a great number of Islamic scholars. He had professional positions in four different religious schools simultaneously. Shams was a wandering dervish, who had spent a lifetime as a mystic journeying within and beyond himself.

Rumi's encounter with Shams, is believed by some to be one of the most amazing incidents in the development and expansion of human self-awareness. This encounter was destined to expand Rumi to a creative dimension far beyond what any ordinary person is able to reach. Within the short time that the two of them spent together, immersed in spiritual discussions, Rumi was completely changed from a religious leader into a poet of great madness, who was dancing and singing ecstatic songs of love as he wandered through the alleys and streets.

If Rumi had not met Shams and had not developed such a powerful love for him, the world would not have had the opportunity to benefit from the creative expression of the great mystic he eventually became. Through the power of love, a man, who had never written a poem in his life, became one of the most celebrated poets of all times, giving rise to the extraordinary outpouring of some of the greatest love sonnets. He describes his encounter with Shams in such a delicate way:

In the midst of the darkness,
a moon appeared with its brilliance.
Stepping down from the clouds, it glanced at me.
Like a skillful falcon
that hunts a bird and steals it away,
it captured me and flew back to infinite space.
As I looked for myself,
I could not find me, for my body
had become all soul in the tenderness of love.
The nine spheres of heaven
dissolved in that moon as the ship of
my existence drowned in the sea of love.

The creative process can be experienced almost as another person with whom we interact, a presence which we come to know. We begin to have conversations with our unborn creations. We can ask it questions, and it will give us intelligible answers. Like loving someone, commitment to the creative act is commitment to the unknown as well as befriending what is unknowable. It helps us to understand the need for faith in reaching for it.

Love is much more than pleasure and joy. It is a reaching for what is unknown. Love invites the expression of art from us in order to see itself. We reach out beyond the known edges of self to unite with the beloved, to touch, to sense, to reshape, to rejuvenate, and to create new life.

Love offers itself for the sake of love, for the edifying and ecstatic experience of transcendence. Whenever we love what we are creating, we subconsciously enhance its beauty, and bring more music, poetry and dance to it. Love lifts us from the cross of our own crucifixion, and comforts, soothes and anoints us with sacred oils to set us free. Creation offers the gifts of beauty and nurture in every moment, an anointing of its own kind. Nature itself is in a perpetual cycle of seasons to give us spring.

There is a fountain of youth: it is your mind, your talents, the creativity
you bring to your life and the lives of people you love.
When you learn to tap this source, you will truly have defeated age.

SOPHIA LOREN

The palace of dreams within our perception looks for the kingdom of the beloved, for the house of the beloved, in a search of love. The only thing that remains is that place where we dwell with love in the soul. Everything becomes an enticement, a lure, and everything else that is blocking love is destroyed and ruined to clear the way. It is useless to run away from the challenge of love. In the end, love is the only companion that can bring us joy.

We can question ourselves. Are we the lover or the beloved? Do we really need this, or do we just want it? Is this necessary? We can live without many things, but not without love. It is not really living if we are trying to avoid the greatest of all possible experiences in this life. It is truly a grace to know that it is love that attracts us. It is then and only then, that we know we are moving in a direction toward the fullness of life.

The power of love warns and teaches us to recognize the clues of love, so that we become awake and aware enough to hear only our own heart. It is the only true guidance we are given. Our heart knows us better than we know ourselves. Listen to it! What is it that sings to you in the quiet moments?

When the sun rises at dawn, creation reveals its face to us. Love is like the sun that brightens our life at dawn as our beloved appears in the light. Our heart opens and takes the beloved in, and the energy of love gives a new radiance to our creations. Colors of paintings grow brighter, forms become more delicate, and brushstrokes become softer. Love takes over, and lover and beloved unite. Anything we create becomes the expression of love, and we feel united with our creation. We become the altar of creation itself. We dance because our heart is dancing. We let beauty have its way with us.

One can climb mountains on a quest, cross the desert looking for the truth, seek the advice of kings and prophets, but the truth can only be found in one's own heart. It is written there through secret longings in a language that only lovers can hear. A dream lover can make us feel wonderful for a night, but disappears when we go to work. The beloved never leaves us. The beloved goes to work with us and whispers love songs in our ear during class, in lectures and in the middle of final exams.

To experience the harmony of love and creativity working together is the ultimate goal of humankind. The union of the two becomes the nature of our belief about our creator. As human beings, we have been created to experience our own creative nature. However, there are seductive passions and goals that can limit our creative power. Only those who are freed from the goals that limit them, whose hearts are filled with love, discover the opportunities to move forward and claim the divine nature from which they came. When we create without love, our creations are austere and without spirit.

If we don't combine our love with creative expression in some way, it will lack the flow of excitement and then life becomes a matter of meeting needs and obtaining necessities. This can quickly extinguish the fire of love. Creativity is the thread that guides love, the song of the soul that uncovers us. Friedrich Nietzsche wrote, *"And those who were seen dancing were thought to be insane by those who could not hear the music."*

Many artists and creative people have faced depression in their lives. Some have even committed suicide while at the height of their success. What is missing in their lives is the elevating energy of love, which is the best antidepressant in existence. Love is as critical to our mind and body as oxygen. The less we experience love in our life, the more likely we are to become depressed.

The artists who face depression are often those who are unable to love themselves, and they do not feel loved by others. They often become very self-focused, which makes them even less attractive to others, further depriving them of opportunities to develop the energizing power of love. One reason we may become depressed is that we sit around passively waiting for someone to show up with the love we need, but love doesn't work that way. To experience love and to attract love, we need to already be in love. We need to be in love with life and with everything around us and be actively expressing that love in a variety of creative ways.

To be free in the expression of love is to always be open to receiving it anywhere at any time without any conscious effort. As love begins to radiate from those who are able to do this, they will generate and receive even more love from others, which stimulates the flow of creative juices inside of them. The stirring of love naturally offers an experience of joy to everyone around them. This becomes a path towards understanding the true nature of the self in relation to one's environment, which is the deeper meaning of the idea expressed in scripture that *man is created in the image of God*. The entire universe is created through a mysteriously divine substance that is infinite love, and we are already immersed in it. As a society, we have failed to help awaken others to this truth. Hopefully, we can come together to raise the awareness of this challenging invitation of love.

We are descendants of divine light. The image of the creator is always shining within us. This is the revelation from which all physical life is made, and it flows from this divine light. Like the source of all light, it carries with it the potential of inner creative intelligence and power, and we exist on Earth to make creative use of it. Recognizing this truth helps us to develop a more inclusive love for all that has been created. Everything is made of a divine substance, and we are given the power of imagination and creativity to use it for the benefit of all creation! It is not given to us for ourselves alone. We damage it by personalizing it and using it only for our own satisfaction, especially when we use it to wield power over others to satisfy the ego.

If we pour love into what we create, we can reflect more consciously on what we are reaching for. Rather than focusing on what we receive through the creating process, we surrender to the flow of what is being created through us, just as we surrender to a partner in expressing and sharing love. We follow the flow of love as it guides us in all relationships and in our interaction with life. Of course this is a challenging process for many people to learn, especially those who have not transcended their own wants and needs to be able to consider another in the same way as they do themselves. Many creative people are so focused on their own process that they are not able to move beyond self-involvement enough to be able to surrender to and be guided by love. The more sensitive we are to others and the more we learn to respond to their needs, the more we are able to tap into the source of creativity that is available to every one of us.

How do we awaken to the beautiful reality that all that flows through the universe is meant for all of us, instead of limiting and narrowing our world to reach only for our own selfish concerns? This is the power of love, the energy that already exists, waiting to guide us on a journey of companionship and creative expression. This is the undiscovered power that has yet to be recognized as an incredible gift flowing from the source of all creation. If I am to bear witness to anything in my life, it is to be a living testament to the truth of the power of love that is freely given for every man, woman, child, and every form of life on Earth. When we surrender to love, we let it take us where it will. We surrender into a guiding energy that instinctively knows the ways of love.

Art is much more than the appearance of form and the artist is much more than someone who learns to copy a likeness of something else. In our highest and deepest moments, *we are the creators of our own existence,* and creation itself is attracted to our energy when we respond with love. We are called to share our stories, to create new visions, to risk the unraveling of the veils and masks we hide behind, and when we do, we give the deeper feelings within our hearts the chance to flower and grow into a pure freedom to create something new. We let our hearts guide us into new ways of seeing and anoint us with a glowing light from within, for the longing within our hearts attracts love as the sacred alchemy that transforms our life experience into joy. If all the legends of the Holy Grail conceal a hidden essence of truth, it is found in the emanations of the radiant mystery of the heart.

POWER OF HEART

Your vision will become clear only when you look into your heart.
Who looks outside, dreams. Who looks inside, awakens.

CARL JUNG

TO LOOK AT CREATION WITH open eyes, one would only see the surface and all that covers it. To see beyond the senses, there is a need for one who knows the way. The heart is such a guide. It is a wise and wonderful guide that is within a person as a beloved friend who can always be trusted to lead the way to the truth. When creations are simply seen through the outer eyes, it is impossible to embark on the journey of enlightenment taken through the heart.

The heart has long been used as a metaphor for the moral, emotional, and spiritual core of humanity. In the past, it was also considered to be the center of intellectual understanding and was widely believed to be the location of the human mind. More than thirteen hundred years ago, the revelations of the Quran indicated that the heart possesses intelligence, and revealed that it thinks as well as it feels. In the mummification process, all the organs were removed except for the heart, as the Egyptians considered it to be the center of intelligence and emotion. In poetic language the word 'heart' is used in reference to the soul. Stylized depictions of the heart are the most prevalent symbols of love in the history of the world.

Within the past decade or so, the heart has become the center of much attention. Even in the business world, the mission statement of many companies is now emphasizing the importance of considering the heart in customer care and leadership. Today, many motivational speakers, books and articles advise us to connect, listen and follow the heart as a basis for major decision making. Utilizing the power of the heart to enhance creativity and to stimulate more compassion and care is needed now more than ever.

Many believe that conscious awareness originates in the brain alone. Recent scientific research suggests that consciousness actually emerges from the brain and body acting together. A growing body of evidence suggests that the heart plays a particularly significant role in this process. Research in neuroradiology indicates that the heart is a sensory organ that receives and processes information. It continuously sends signals to the brain that influence our emotion, perception and cognition. The heart generates an electromagnetic field that is sixty times greater and has a magnetic component that is five thousand times stronger than the brain.

The creative process usually starts with balancing feelings and activating the power of the heart. When we are able to practice emotional management of the heart, we reach the highest level of creativity, which is recreating our perceptions of reality. Whatever our circumstances may be, or whatever our past has been, the power that determines our future is within our own heart and mind. It is here that the star of our destiny truly shines.

It is confusing, disorienting and often frightening to turn away from a comfortable way of being to step into the unknown spaces of our own souls. Yet, it is in the primitive caves of the unknown, the depths of the sea of longing, the unknown regions of space, and in the wilderness of what has not yet been created, that we step into an expanding universe, instead of the one collapsing in on itself. The heart holds the mystery of the cave of the unknown. Creative people are those who dare to explore the unknown and return to share what they have seen and experienced.

Creating through the power of the heart requires us to return to the instinctive feelings that arise when we are in our own integrity and act out of that energy. Even when we use our mind to make what we have created presentable, we must remain focused on the feeling and not allow our thoughts to take precedence. The intellect will follow the action set in motion by the heart.

The expression of love is the way the heart offers itself for the edifying and ecstatic experience of transcendence and transformation. The burdens we carry around take many forms, but they consist of our own projections of what we think and what we fear. What concerns us and what we worry about gathers energy that materializes as a very heavy load that we drag around wherever we go. The heart guides us and lifts us tenderly from the cross of our own making and frees us from our own personal crucifixion and judgment, to comfort, soothe and anoint us with the sacred oils of love.

Prior to leaving my home for America as a teenager, I asked my mystic uncle how to find the way, since I was going to be away from his valuable spiritual guidance. He told me that every time I needed help to choose a direction in my life or to make an important decision, I should first use the rational mind to organize the available choices into two distinct categories, and then let my heart choose the one that is right for me. He said if I use my heart like a compass, the path would surely become clear to me. Since then, whenever making a decision is difficult or is draining my energy, I turn to my heart and allow the powerful inner guidance to align me.

Creativity allows the gifts of beauty and nurture to unfold in every moment. This is an anointing of another kind. The perpetual cycle of nature means the renewal of spring is always ahead of us, much like a loving servant who gives all he can to nurture the one he serves. Creating is the ultimate guide to living a joyous life, as it becomes a generous gift from one heart to another. Abundance flows from the earth, from those who love us, and from the natural cycle of the cosmos that bless us every day. When we take all that we have for granted and never realize the incredible gifts of this life, we miss the beauty of perceiving the creatorship behind those gifts.

There is a path of light flowing through the heart that opens our awareness of the existence of others. Our fears can hold us hostage and isolate and separate us from the love that longs to unite us. We mistakenly think that only other people can tell us what is right, that we should be what they think we should be, or that things should appear the way others think they should look. It is not through looking with the outer eyes that we discover the truth, but through observing in an interior way. We perceive the truth within our own hearts. This is our personal and intimate experience of revelation.

One of the most profound events that greatly affected my art is related to what happened when I took figure painting during my second year of fine arts in college. A beautiful girl posed nude throughout the course. I took the class with the intention of receiving a high grade, for by then, painting nude figures was my specialty. During each session, after I finished my own painting, I would assist other students with their works. When mid-term grades came out, I was shocked to find out I had a "D" for the course. I complained to the instructor about the grade and he told me if I wanted to have a better grade I had to learn how to paint. Mockingly, I asked him to teach me painting.

During the next session, the instructor told me to make an imaginary cross-section through the model's neck and paint what I could perceive in my imagination. While looking at the model, I painted what I remembered from biology classes about bones, muscles, skin, esophagus, epiglottis and veins. During the following session, he told me to make another imaginary cross-section; this time through her chest and paint what I could visualize. Again, I used my knowledge of anatomy and painted the skin, the chest bones, the ligaments, the lungs and the heart.

At the start of the third session, I asked the instructor what to paint next and he placed his finger on the heart that I had painted and told me to paint what is inside it. This was a different way of painting for me. I kept on staring at the model, but I was not seeing what was in front of my eyes. I was trying to reach inside the model's heart to see what was going on in there. Sometimes, I thought she must be very uncomfortable posing naked in front of the students. Following that thought, my colors became dark and muddy, reflecting what I imagined was the model's uncomfortable feeling. Next, I thought she must enjoy posing naked for the class, and my colors changed to bright pinks, reds and vibrant oranges.

This process went on for several sessions, and I kept on changing my painting and its colors. I was looking at the nude model more and more, yet seeing her physical being less and less. Finally, after a long struggle of trying to find out what was inside the model's heart, I realized it was not about her heart. It was about my heart and what was going through it as I was painting. That breakthrough guided me to paint through the vision and feelings that arise within me. There was no more judgment about whether anything on the canvas was right or wrong, or whether or not it was proportional. For the first time, I had created a work of art through the perceptive experience of my own heart, and those who looked at it, saw it through their hearts.

After spending many years developing painting techniques, I finally began to learn to create art that comes from the heart and not from the prescribed mental process of reproducing the way something looks. More importantly, I learned that works of art should be experienced through emotions.

To lead a life in which we are inspired and able to inspire others, our hearts have to be alive and filled with passion and enthusiasm. To achieve that, we must have the courage to be true to our own experience of life. Rather than borrowing from or imitating others, we need the conviction of being able to think and feel for ourselves and to take action to develop our own sense of responsibility for what we express. Deaf and blind American author, educator and a leading humanitarian activist, Helen Keller said, *"The best and most beautiful things in the world cannot be seen or even touched; they must be felt with the heart."*

To live creatively, we must welcome all intentions and actions that express a certain quality to the heart, and integrate the experiences into our daily life. These qualities include the appreciation or care of others, the expression of kindness to those around us, the development of ideas and ways to work with those who relieve the suffering of others, and the preservation and protection of the planet's resources. When we create through the heart, we become less self-centered, and we don't feel so separate. Hopefully, we would form fewer judgments, become more aware, be better able to follow our intuition, and learn to be more discerning.

The heart is the portal to great fulfillment, which takes place on an interior level first. When we use our hearts to shift perception and direct the flow of our emotions, we are able to generate and magnetize our own process toward fulfillment. Physical satisfaction does not last in the same way as inner fulfillment. We have all seen people who thought being rich would bring them fulfillment, only to find that even with great wealth they remain unhappy.

To follow the heart is to rely on our intuitive feelings and to surrender to the process of discovering what is truly meaningful to us. It is to care enough about the integrity of our own experience to allow it to happen. It is not about following our thoughts and what we think needs to be done. It relies on intuition, is guided by the muse and is vigilant about keeping whatever we are doing aligned with the deeper feelings of the heart.

Every creative experience in life is initiated from the flow of energy. If we stay focused on the feeling of the flow, we will not become distracted by our rational mind as it tries to recreate what it already knows and has experienced. We learn to follow our intuition and surrender to what we feel is right by staying focused on our heart's desire. This is not an easy task, for we continuously become distracted by our thoughts. Our rational mind wants to interject judgment and whatever it thinks is the right thing to do. By eliminating the imposition of past experiences, we can remain focused on our feelings, because the mind can only recreate the past as thought.

The reason we need to stay clear of thought as the primary catalyst while we are creating, is that our mind wants to impose what it already believes on our behavior, rather than allowing what is infused and hidden within us to be unveiled. The mind instinctively wants to be in control, rather than in surrender. Hafiz, in his poetic language, describes how, after creating the universe, God noticed he had not truly manifested the wholeness of his being. To do so, he took a handful of dust from the earth, and spent forty days and nights manifesting his own nature into it. He called that handful of dust, 'the heart.'

When the universal consciousness became aware of the special energy of the divine presence in the form of the heart, jealousy entered the creation experience and it aroused the desire to destroy it. God had the angels create the body of Adam and he placed 'the heart' inside of it.

As soon as Adam, the first man, became aware of the divine power inside of him, he decided to take advantage of this and use it to benefit himself. To prevent that, the divine hand of the creator severed the connection between the mind and the heart, so the mind would not be aware that the very nature of God was dwelling inside of him, beating a divine rhythm within his own heart. According to Hafiz, all the religious wars are due to our not knowing or realizing that our heart is the manifestation or incarnation of God. We continue to search for God outside of ourselves, but all this time he has been dwelling within us.

As people of the twenty-first century, we are seriously in need of a different approach to our unity as a response to what is quickly becoming a global community. We need to find an approach that allows us to connect with each other through our hearts. It starts with each individual connecting with their own heart and letting it open a path to making more conscious choices through love as the way of uniting us with each other. When we are able to develop the unique path that we were created to follow, it strengthens our intention to move toward the beloved.

When we connect directly with our own heart, we simultaneously become connected to the amazing power of creativity, sometimes gruff, sometimes blunt, sometimes we cut through everything to reflect the brilliant rays of light that guide us in the ways of the heart. It can be a lion's roar, and certainly not the faint whimper of the weakness of self-involvement and self-focus.

Alignment with the heart guides each person toward the manifestation of love. In some ways, the heart becomes a metaphor for the great mystic in each one of us. It nudges us to wake up and face the unknown spaces waiting for us to create! Throughout my artistic career, I have heard and received heart reactions to many of my paintings as others reveal how they were guided, invited, awakened, and aroused by them. I realize that is because those feelings reflect the same longings that were happening within me while I was creating the artworks.

As I began to inspire others to become involved with their own creative process, I could see how those who responded to the invitation felt awakened to what was already within them. It became clear that it was not something that only artists possess and the ordinary person doesn't. I realized I was touching on something that gives each person access to their own inner teacher. My students began to learn how to listen to that guide inside of them, to feel the approaching presence, to clear the mind, open the heart and welcome the coming of spirit. I witnessed the artist within coming alive over and over again.

To unite with each other through connecting with the heart, we need to learn to discern when it is the ego coming in disguise, and when it is time to be vulnerable, from when it is not. The jump the heart makes when the beloved approaches could be described as a quantum leap. When we bound forward to welcome the beloved, we receive and transform the seeds of light, and birth them through creative expression to share the gift of our heart's evolution. The creative souls here on earth, who are connected with the heart, help to guide others through their heart energy. These souls emanate a vibration of love that can be felt in their voice and through the senses, and can become a point of alignment for others. They may not even be aware of the effect and how powerful the connection can be. Yet, if a spiraling cycle of energy is formed between two hearts, there is a continuing flow of the spirit of love from one being to another. The heart is a welcoming sanctuary for the beloved, and welcomes this most precious of all connections.

The secret entrance to the soul is known to the heart, and when that is realized, one can move freely between the dimensions we once believed were separate. When each person opens to this, the beloved, who carries the imprint of the energy of the heart, will draw them together with empowering energy. We become attracted to one another, as kindred spirits, for the purpose of fully developing the pathway for creative energy.

The heart's messages flow between people through energy, images, songs, voice, wind, clouds, breeze and breath from heart to heart, and deep in the unconscious, from soul to soul. No wonder it scares and humbles us. No wonder it makes us shiver and shake and roar and cry and want to pull a cover over our heads, or run and jump in the nearest lake or pool to cool off. When new islands are being formed through volcanic activity in the ocean, we can hear the sizzling heat and see the rising steam of the fire of creation at work. When we love and create it is at work within us as well!

People ask me which of my paintings is my favorite, and I always respond that it is the one I am working on, because new insights come whenever I create. I feel so alive when I am creating. When people ask me to name my favorite book or which is my favorite chapter in the book, I say it is the one I am working on, because creating opens the heart to its treasures.

The heart has great significance for everyone in determining the value of their life and their relationships, and there are no words powerful enough to express the importance of the heart experience in this world. It is the longing, the wish, and the hope of every human being to come alive to the gift of the power of the heart that is able to embrace each moment with the great love out of which it was created.

Joy is an incredibly energizing, life-giving, and ecstatic overflowing of the love hidden in the heart. There is a divine light within the heart, which spreads out to surround the space around it. When the heart is set free, that light elevates us beyond words, makes us translucent and glowing, and infuses us with the spirit of love. Through that light, I wave my paint brush like a ray of the sun and paint each life with the beauty I feel in my heart!

POWER OF UNIQUENESS

At bottom every man knows well enough that he is a unique being, only once on this earth; and by no extraordinary chance will such a marvelously picturesque piece of diversity in unity as he is, ever be put together a second time.

FRIEDRICH NIETZSCHE

THE WORLD IS CREATED OUT of varied and unique elements. Every human being is physically, mentally, emotionally and spiritually unique. Personal feelings, thoughts and habits are as diverse as finger prints. Everyone sees life through the lens of their own unique experience, beliefs and perspective. We identify each other as having unique qualities or characteristics that enable us to tell each other apart. We label people as funny, sloppy, friendly, as someone with a mustache, who is tall or short with blue eyes, and use many different words to describe each other.

Uniqueness is significant and definitely has an effect on a person's life. It might affect someone's success, whether they are able to meet their goals in life, or it may influence whether or not their dreams are realized. Uniqueness is often determined by other people's opinions or by the way people imagine us to be, whether we agree with how they see us or not.

Although all people are in one group as the human race, each person is distinct and unique with different patterns and vibrations of energy in the way they live in the world. It is interesting that when someone recognizes or acknowledges this uniqueness, there is a feeling of being seen and known on a deeper level.

Uniqueness holds a key to discovering the emotions of people. The connection a viewer experiences with a work of art is often decided on the basis of how it makes them feel, even though justification or evaluation tends to come through in rational description. Great works like the Parthenon, the Sistine Chapel, or Beethoven's Ninth evoke immediate feelings and recognition of uniqueness.

History is filled with the names of those who became successful and well known for their extraordinary creativity and innovative ideas that helped to change the view of the world in some way. Impressionism, for instance, developed as a departure from what had been accepted as the more traditional and classical technique, and it helped to free artists to express themselves in a way that was unique to them. Monet expressed his personality and his perceptions through his unique interpretation of colors and light, as well as his brushstrokes. The way he structured them on canvas became a creative outburst that spread throughout the art world as the blossoming visions of Monet's unique perspective and nature.

Creative people, who break free from conventional approaches, help us to take the time to learn who we are, to pay attention to how we feel, and to discover unique ways of expressing ourselves to others. Artists learn to develop abilities, talents, and gifts to be able to share with others what matters to them. Studying the techniques and works of different artists helps us to learn what it is that makes each one so unique. It also helps us to find our own uniqueness and our own form of expression. The purpose is not to imitate anyone or follow their path, but to help us discover our own.

Uniqueness comes through when rules and restrictions are lifted and there are no set guidelines or requirements to follow. When the soul expresses itself through the physical body, it comes through as feeling. When a person is creating, they play with what is available to them at the time, and they let their feelings guide the play. When someone is writing, they play with words, and let them flow freely through the pen. If a person is painting, they play with colors and paint, and let the brush move them freely across the canvas.

As playfulness continues, another aspect of uniqueness develops, which is to encounter a touchable reality. This occurs when uniqueness develops within the creative process. The person enters the rational world of organizing, editing and revising to put what they have created into a form that others will recognize and enjoy. In doing so, they use concepts of beauty and vision that have become their own measure of excellence. It is in that touchable reality that artists develop their unique styles. The refinement is still playful and enjoyable, but a certain standard of the chosen medium helps to express it. This is true whether the person is creating sandcastles on the beach, taking up gourmet cooking, or painting a work of art.

Creativity is a catalyst that develops an insatiable desire to keep on creating. Conversely, conforming to what others are choosing or doing what they expect can easily destroy the desire to create. If society consistently imposes expectations on its members, then technically, we will function as a unit and no one would even care if our guiding muse is imprisoned and silenced. The interesting thing about the idea of following standards is that total uniformity may make a team work together more harmoniously, but it destroys originality and spontaneity in learning who we are and who we might become. Uniformity can easily destroy imagination, and perception ceases to exist, for it is very likely to be destroyed when we are told not to daydream and not to fantasize. According to John F. Kennedy, *"We cannot expect that all nations will adopt similar systems, for conformity is the jailer of freedom and the enemy of growth."*

The first job I held after receiving my architectural degree was at an established architectural firm in Los Angeles. I was to do mostly drafting, for which I had to use the thick book of architectural standards. After several months of continually following the typical standards and requirements of the profession, I was desperate to find a place to play! The best way for me to play, within the confinement of building standards, was to enter architectural design competitions. I divided my time into two time zones, daytime to follow standards in the office, and night time to design buildings at home for competitions.

I entered as many architectural competitions as I could, one after another, and I was rejected in every one of them. Although failures were disappointing, I continued, because my drive to create something in freedom was more important to me than to win a contest. Entering those competitions gave me the opportunity to create without restrictions, through which I developed my own unique approach in architectural design, albeit only on paper. I learned that even when I am confined to work within given frameworks, it is vital to begin by letting my imagination soar and explore new ideas without limitation. During these periods of complete freedom of expression, I was able to make contact with my most authentic and unique creative power.

Creativity develops in three phases. During the first phase, a person learns about the available instruments and techniques. There is no need to reinvent the wheel to design an automobile. We build with what is available and become familiar with the use of special instruments and techniques of our trade in order to develop technical ability.

The second phase is to develop one's own special style. Here, in order to succeed, we have to let go of the techniques we have learned from others, and tap into our own source of identity. Many artists subconsciously transform what they have developed in the first phase, into something personal and unique. The majority of successful and professional artists are functioning in this phase of their creative development.

The third phase of developing creativity is when a person forgets the learned techniques as well as their identity and just plays to inspire and envision new possibilities. Here, we have to forget the past and ignore what has been created up to this point. If we try to stay with our old identity, it causes us to place a kind of unconscious time stamp on our style, which is the antithesis and enemy of creativity. We don't need to draw inspiration from what we have done previously, nor do we even need to consider it.

Some artists try to fit their works into a category or a certain genre in order to attract a growing patronage. This may be profitable, but it can also be severely limiting, and it can be a real detriment in developing creative power. Trying to fit into a category, or to follow trends within a style we have developed, is something I always advise artists to stay away from. It is true that labeling the work of art as being in a certain genre is a necessary thing for people to be able to find and identify the artist's work, especially on the internet. However, it should not be fixed in the mind of the artist during the creative process. Styles, methods or genre really do not matter when it comes to developing one's unique style of expression.

The nature of creativity has to do with wanting to share feelings with others. We are usually eager to learn about other people's reactions to what we have created. The problem we face here is that feedback is invariably given with preconceived notions of what the outcome should be. Criticism, whether it is negative or positive, will unconsciously push us in a direction that someone else sees as best for us. Unfortunately, rather than trusting our muse or being free enough to have fun and experiment, we can end up doing what brings us approval. It might be done with the best of intentions, but it can actually harm our capacity to use the inner senses in developing our own creativity. Of course, this is different from sharing our work for the benefit of others, but is not helpful if we truly want to find our own path of creative expression. Once we are done with our creative work, whatever it may be, it is then a much more appropriate time to listen to feedback. We need to be careful not to pay attention to criticism while we are actually creating, for it can place a restraint on our freedom to express our uniqueness.

The hardest part about uniqueness is often our own recognition of it. It is not something that we can contrive or generate just because we want to be different or special. We can't just work at it to make ourselves be something we're not. Many artists have discovered their originality through what seems to be a happy accident, but when we pay closer attention and stay aware, we find out that it develops through loving what we do and who we are. We suddenly realize that creative uniqueness is born. We give birth to it as our heart overflows with the energy of love and joy, simply by being and living in that flow. That which makes us expand and explode into a blossoming expression of our deeper nature is a revelation to ourselves as well as to others who see the light streaming from us. This is the mysterious glow of falling in love with the mystery of life itself.

When an individual continues to create works which focus on a similar subject or theme, they are able to see an overview and actually behold a style developing in their creative work. This causes them to recognize the power of creativity, originality, and how it affects them as well as others. They learn to identify the patterns and preferences that help to establish the foundation of their uniqueness. Everyone is then motivated to learn to use the medium through which their uniqueness is expressed, whether it is writing, painting, performing, sculpting, singing, making music, dancing, or simply living creatively!

Everyone is free to create, and our creativity is determined by how one can manifest it in the most delightful of ways. We are all born with an inner freedom, and everyone has the creative right to their own domain and to discover the best way to live through it. We have been created to be the monarchs of our own hearts, to reign over the kingdom of the beloved. This only happens if we are able to connect with the heart through the flow of creative energy within each one of us. This is the wonder of developing a relationship with the inner muse that becomes the beloved within us. Uniqueness only truly emerges through a deep sense of being able to love one's true self. There is a secret within the mystery of life that miraculously reveals that we were created out of love. The great power that created the universe tenderly whispers and sings like a breath in the wind, which becomes a divine serenade.

When self-survival and gratification become the only purpose of our creative pursuits, it can be frightening and dark in motive. Everything we do then becomes a way to display the self, to show off, or to use the precious gift of life in a self-serving way. We take advantage of it as a means to sell the self. We forget that everyone has the right to express their capabilities, to have the same opportunity to reveal them, and to share the results with others to experience relationship. This is creative power, and it is a power that is meant to benefit everyone involved, not just a privileged few. This is how we help each other evolve into someone amazing – not by controlling others and trying to influence them to be more like someone else. Developing our uniqueness actually grows out of love, the fertile valley of caring and helping to develop others by stimulating their own creative desire to express love in their own ways.

The beauty of life comes when we are free, especially, when the freedom is found within the boundaries of our personal capacity to express it. We all need to have equal opportunities to express ourselves in order to be seen, heard, and recognized. It is the longing and the territory of the dream that needs to be expanded. When every being knows the feeling of being affirmed and loved, love will become a way of being that enhances the art of living.

We can only feel true unity with others when we feel empowered within ourselves. This allows every person to experience their own creative uniqueness, providing the salt that brings out the flavor that is uniquely ours, and opening the door to a new world where harmony and peace become the primary power. This only happens when we give more of ourselves, our resources, and our time to others, without expectation or demand in return. Living a creative life is its own reward. We discover the treasures hiding within our hearts. According to Oscar Wilde, *"Art is individualism, and individualism is a disturbing and disintegrating force. Therein lies its immense value. For what it seeks is to disturb the monotony of type, slavery of custom, tyranny of habit, and the reduction of man to the level of a machine."*

During the twentieth century, Picasso and Braque showed us how they were able to develop their creative uniqueness through observation. Picasso taught us to see in reverse, to move away from a single point of perception, by moving into the world of the dream and away from the ordinary world of reality. He broke with reality, placed things into cubes, and changed their proportions. Through this process, he taught us about the many ways we can manifest our vision by moving beyond the judgments we make as to whether our creations reveal beauty or ugliness. A pearl can be hidden in the most unlikely places. It is not the container of the pearl that is the treasure. This is a pearl of great price and the essence of something unseen that clears the way for joy and the fullness of life.

In cubism, Picasso and Braque were trying to show how intelligence, the power of mind, and simplicity can all come together in presenting an image. If the goal is simply to make this identifiable to others, it moves into a prescribed complexity, and some who view it try to discover that complexity in order to conform with others who recognize it. Abstract painting sets up a pattern of complexity, so that those who are viewing it try to discover the complexity in order to conform by being able to recognize it. This whole process weakens creative power and imprisons the muse in the artist.

As individuals, we develop categories to identify ourselves, by saying that we are a painter or a plumber. We also develop categories to identify art with all the 'isms' we place at the end of the terms. If we are used to handling the ball of life in a certain way, it is difficult to surrender to the divine accidents that may happen as we learn new ways to do things. We preclude ourselves from the experience of having fun if we always have to come from a fixed point of view. If we cling to a certain way of doing things, it can lead us to a situation where there is no movement or life. A creative movement might well create a little chaos. What happens when we block this flow is that we begin to trade the process for the product, focusing only on the end result. We kill the joy.

Henri Rousseau painted forests and animals so realistically, that when you look at them, you forget where you are. That is true creativity when it touches others in a transcendent way. In order to do this, Rousseau broke out of the mold and the habit of conformity. Always crossing the street between the lines painted on the asphalt, is to conform. Sometimes, we have to take another route, change behavior, and break the rules. It is a creative act to risk taking a different path.

An emerging artist once told me that she was a perfectionist. I asked her to explain what that meant to her, for there is no such a category in my vocabulary. I told her to throw the category away and throw away whatever led her to think that she was a perfectionist. Even if our educational system were to give itself to deepening our spirit and our art, to develop our souls, we would still be in the same place, because we still have to go through the process. It is the process of becoming. We cannot just lift ourselves onto the planet of creativity. We have to experience the moment when innocence turns into experience and when conformity is transformed into creativity. A lover wants to express love in a different way than before to keep it new, to feel love, not just to go through the motions. The beloved would celebrate that, for variation is the heart of creativity, and love is the ultimate creative act. Our hearts long to bring life and variety to the act of creating and especially to our loving relationships, because it is the nature of love to inspire us to live a life of pure joy.

Many artists fall short of having unique experiences, because they are afraid of the unknown and uneasy with what is not familiar. The fear of the unknown can make many shiver and quake when they come face to face with the opportunity to experience raw creative power. Falling into love can be an overwhelming experience that changes everything. When we are in the flow of passion it is new and exciting, there is no style, no school, no institution, and no amount of money that helps us to interact with it. When we interface with it, we do the best we can, however perfectly or imperfectly. By entering into that kind of spontaneity in the creative process, we are somehow marvelously freed from caring about what others think or how they react. It is exhilarating and makes us feel more alive. The more we develop and honor our own expression, the fewer obstacles we encounter as we seek new ways to express our own developing creativity.

The power of uniqueness is an expression of the great diversity and variation of the source of all energy that flows through creation. Each one of us holds our own original place in the universe as a vital part of the amazing tapestry of humanity. How this creative power moves through us depends upon our openness, our desire for it and how brave we are. We use our abilities and experiences to integrate and manifest creatively in our lives in whatever ways we choose to do that.

As artists, we are explorers, seeking out wholeness and balance in the hope of discovering our own unique kind of relationship with the universe, and even more importantly, our relationship with ourselves. When we do this, we feel a rising wonder and a powerful connection with all life. In return, we experience an infusion of joy, a deepening awareness of who we are, and we are blessed through the grace of transformation. Suddenly, the world seems to be welcoming us home! We live in the kingdom of our hearts with the belovedness of our own being!

POWER OF FREEDOM

When I am dead, let it be said of me: he belonged to no school,

to no church, to no institution, to no academy, and least of all,

to any regime except the regime of liberty.

GUSTAVE COURBET

TO HAVE FREEDOM IS TO be delivered from any confinement or restraint. Freedom is being exempt from external control, regulation and interference. It is to be unconstrained by any limitation or restriction imposed by thought, action or the expansion of desire. Free are those who are not enslaved to their own wants.

Freedom is discovered in the process of doing what we truly love to do. It offers constant renewal and opens doors to infinite possibilities. Freedom does not lie in candid expression of individual nature, but in the union of it with the constraints that exist around us. When limitation is treated with love, it loosens the grip of whatever is binding it.

Those who remain slaves to their thoughts tend to build prison walls around themselves in order to be happy. The practice of maintaining a fixed view of the world too easily becomes an obstacle to growth and prevents the experience of true creative expression. Pure love is the key to free those who are slaves to their wants and needs, whether it is their own or the craving of someone who wants something from them for personal satisfaction. Love only thrives in freedom, which is why any substitute for it dies and ends so quickly, draining us of energy instead of renewing it.

Living the creative process is to bring together all that comes from a deeper source, even when we are not aware of them in a conscious way. Fragments of dreams, past experiences and feelings that are carried in cellular memory and more, can connect in creativity and love, as we surrender to the ecstasy of letting dreams mingle with the reality of the present moment. In this process, a footprint or imprint is created that allows love to stream between dreams and reality. When intention is set through faith and surrender, something totally new will be created.

To create is to explore both the known and the unknown possibilities of the spiritual connection between personal experience and acquired knowledge. Creativity is opening to a folding and unfolding of an expanding life, not unlike a heartbeat, or the rising and setting of the sun. The universe is unfolding before us as we live and experience each day. The ocean expresses free movement in the waves as they touch the shore and circle back into its depths. Such freedom is recognized only when it is felt and when that happens, we embrace it by leaping into the spiritual arms of pure love.

Freedom in creating is a playfulness known as *leila*. It is a Sanskrit word that expresses the infinite variation and the rhythm of creation that interfaces with the energies and flows within the process. *Lei* is to create and *la* is to destroy. *Leila* is about making and destroying, with no attachment to the end result, or any particular goal in mind. It is about the freedom of just playing and having fun. As we engage freely in the creative act of expressing ourselves through various artistic mediums, the result is some kind of beauty, a living artwork that we are able to see, hear, play or feel. Love falls into form, anointing our eyes and becoming a companion on our journey.

Surrendering into the creative process is to free the playful child within who has been told to behave in accordance with the expectation of others. As artists, we invite the child to enter the playground where *leila* is the natural way of doing things. It takes many experiences to realize the freedom of becoming the master of our own life. This happens when we utilize our freedom to draw on the imagination, to enlarge and expand on whatever we physically or emotionally experience by embracing it and surrendering to pure love to guide us through what is unseen and unknown to us.

Some artists are naturally attracted to the thrill of the result or outcome of the creative act. Others are drawn to surrender into the movement of creative energy. Whatever we do, we need to enter into the process feeling totally open and free enough to follow the guidance of the muse. Artists who are attached to their style, their reputation, or are looking for success, build a kind of prison around themselves, which limits and prevents them from experiencing the pure joy of creating. In surrendering to this flow a connection with our deeper nature takes place to reveal the deeper truth that can become something fresh and new. Creative transformation can guide us into an entirely new way of experiencing life.

Everyone is creative in some way, but those who catch the fire and find the path of creative energy are often the ones who can bring it to life. When a work of art is created, it becomes attractive to the lover who dwells deep within everyone, waiting and longing to be free. Letting the lover stream into form – and into life – through the movement of our own creative expression is a wondrous experience!

For some people, the pleasure of creative power and presentation fuse together into a free-flowing manifestation. For others, the power of the presentation becomes a much more overwhelming focus. It is difficult to say if it is the spiritual energy that is moving through the artist, or if the physical energy of the artist is reflecting it. One without the other leaves no way to distinguish between the two. Dualism that separates one aspect from another is divisive and steals the beauty and variation of the multi-dimensional depth of creation itself.

In the creative act, the beauty and the beast meet each other and unite. The beast allows us to appreciate the beauty, and the beauty lures us to confront the beast with love. Together they plunge us into the magic of transformation to face the fullness of who we are and how we face the truth. The source of all union is to bring two opposites together by fusing and blending the differences into wholeness, and hopefully to preserve the distinctive individuality of both at the same time. If we are unable to do that, the richness and diversity of creation becomes sterilized, and it turns into some bland and generic version of deceptive idealism. We recognize when this happens because it leaves us feeling empty and wondering where the magic has gone!

There is a primary meaning of the word 'freedom' that has nearly been lost in modern democratic societies. Today's world, in general, defines freedom as the ability to be free to do what we want to do or to express what we want to express without having any constraints. There is another side of freedom that is considered to be the province of the spirit, and that involves having an inner freedom that we sense and experience within.

True freedom is not limited by physical constraints or psychological and mental pressure. When we embrace physical and spiritual freedom together, we discover the real joy and sweetness of being free. Freedom moves us beyond the boundaries, beyond our own self-focus, beyond our desire to control others, and it leads us through the heart into the openness of love. Freedom offers the possibility of creating a heaven on earth by allowing pure love to guide us into the art of living!

When people are asked about their most exalting experiences, they often recall moments where they were free to create. We are all desirous of having the freedom to be able to express the longing for love we feel inside. Instead of allowing love to guide us into the fullness of creative expression, we want to own something that will give us a quick fix or entertain us. We want to have it, and sometimes this is partly because our friends have it. We want a car as a possession, the best and the classiest, instead of just having a means of transportation. That can get us into trouble by entangling us in having to develop the financial means to obtain as well as to protect our belongings. We become a consumer, chained to what we own.

Next time you watch children playing, notice how they play with whatever comes into their hands. They are in the most natural and original stages of childhood, which in the beginning is not about owning and having. They play with a piece of paper that makes a noise, a leftover empty box or some colored yarn, and find delight in their interaction with things.

Our play is very closely related to the flow as well as our own evolution. It heightens our excitement to evolve. Comparison can bring a new dimension into it, and other people may stimulate our evolution by playing with us. That interaction expands our play, until we begin to bring too much thinking into it, or feel like someone else is doing it better than us, and then we start to feel we are missing something that will make us seem more important.

When animals play, like squirrels in the yard, or new kittens, they seem to constantly run, leap, roll on the ground, and chase each other. Creation offers us a playground where we can discover an unbounded flow in everything we do in life. Our work is enhanced if we find something we love to do and bring the joy of creativity into it. Even the way we walk changes if we are heading toward something that excites us.

The enemy we face wells up from inside, is discovered in our fears, and assumes many forms, which we may experience as rejection, depression, anger, cruelty, or greed. We try to control others and our surroundings to eliminate what frightens us in our perception of ourselves and others. The negative energies develop, and cause us to lose our joyfulness. When the child escapes from the freedom of the playground, we lose the child that knows how to *leila* and dance with an unfolding universe. When that happens to us, our world narrows, and the variety in our life is diminished and grows smaller and smaller. We choose to feel safer by eliminating our choices and remaining with familiar options that feel secure. We stop expanding our abilities, and our capabilities become more and more limited. The clouds of fear obscure the light, and we begin to feel nostalgic and passive.

Being free in our playfulness is not about what we do, but how we choose to do it. The beauty of play and the act of creative expression itself does not follow a prescribed path. When Michelangelo was hired by Pope Julius II to paint the ceiling of the Sistine Chapel, his commission was originally to depict a series of figures of the twelve apostles on the ceiling. After the scaffolding was constructed, he started his commission and painted two of the apostles, but it was very difficult for him to follow his patron's instruction, especially because he had to paint the apostles within the limitation of the triangular spaces of the vaulted ceiling. He soon became so frustrated and restrained that one night he took the hatchet, destroyed the entire fresco and ran away from Rome to hide from the Pope's asserted influence.

One day, while he was cutting through rocks in the mountains, he saw a cloud formation that inspired him and made him think of the beginning of the world as described in Genesis. Excited with his inspiration, he went back to the Pope with an entirely new and much more ambitious proposal to paint the 'creation' on the Sistine Chapel ceiling. After the Pope agreed with his idea, he requested to have the chapel draped so he would be able to paint freely and away from any particular guidance or instruction. Thus, in total freedom, he created about three-hundred figures that blended freely with the architecture of the chapel, and the visual story of creation on the ceiling became one of the greatest artworks of all times.

Moving a brush across the canvas can be painstakingly serious, or it can be a journey of discovery. How we hold the brush reveals something about how we will express ourselves. We learn to let the creative energy guide it, instead of allowing our minds to control it with some kind of a pre-established idea of what we want to happen. We are open to beauty, and we perceive it and feel it, and we become more aware of it. The energy flows out in front of us and manifests in form. The images appearing on the canvas and the sounds that flow through us can be a total surprise, and we experience delight in being a part of the flow of creation.

Creation is constantly seeking and creating new ways to manifest itself. We learn to allow ourselves to be open to that flow and to delight in that stream. Only when we ignore or forget all the rules that can possibly limit us, will our creativity truly blossom. If we can just experience it, even in a small way, we will feel and know how real and wonderful it can be. Watch a farmer or a gardener separating seeds for planting with the excitement and anticipation of what will grow from them. Watch a cook in the kitchen, enjoying the textures, color and arrangement of the food. There is a feeling of spontaneity and freedom in the entire process from preparation through completion.

If the creative process is guided by the heart, we *leila* to create with a purity of emotion. Love surrounds us and welcomes the energies that express it. If we begin to worry, we allow fear into the process. When playfulness is minding the door, it dances and charms those who would interfere. We learn not to hand over our freedom to someone who wants to control us. Creativity thrives in an environment of freedom and spontaneous choice.

Whenever an emerging artist asks me if I see any future for them in the art world, I say if they can ask that question, there probably isn't a future for them, because we are the ones whose longing makes it happen! We create the journey that guides us there. The sharing of our creation becomes an intention, and we move with it, reading the clues, and following the flow. Others are attracted to our expressions and the colors of our feelings, which arouse the desire to learn how to express their own creations more clearly. We feel it inside, and we seek the most effective way to guide them onto the canvas. We call for the child, we play the fool, and we let the jester entertain us, make us laugh, and lure us into creating.

If we can keep playing, we preserve the freshness and one surprise leads to another – and we also preserve our freedom. If we start looking for books and seeking advice on how to do everything, we forget how to play our way to a creative result. No one is going to teach us joy. We may be attracted to foolishness and fun, but the secret is to find the path that opens the beauty within ourselves.

When we *leila*, we fall into a garden of possibilities, and we radiate the wonder of it to others. They might plead with us to show them how to do it, and we might be tempted to try. It only truly happens, when we are able to free the child within us to help us remember. If a certain approach isn't working, we tear it down and try a new way. We build a sand castle, and we pour water over it and watch it dissolve, and the sand invites us to make a new one, a more exciting one than before, and the fun is in the discovery!

We can spend our lives protecting our few brief hours of splendor, and we forget that it can happen again and again in new ways. A child does a drawing and then looks for a clean sheet of paper to do another. When playing with clay, they enjoy smashing it as much as making it. We sometimes try to hold on to our moments, and it is then that we can get stuck. A person begins to age when they turn only to their memories and stop creating new ones.

If how we feel about ourselves is dependent upon how others feel about us, we are in a threshing machine that will grind the life out of whatever we do. If we don't find a way to uncover and release what makes us grow and blossom, we will simply be spinning wheels going through the motions. We can complicate the simplest thing by worrying too much about how we should do it. *Leila* beckons us to do it upside down, right side up, or foolishly, turning it inside out to experience the fun of it. We begin to enjoy the dance. We can see the energy in the movement. We become the musician that plays without a score, improvises and lets the music play through him.

There are so many voices flowing through us, so many faces revealing themselves, so many feelings affecting us, and we choose which ones to develop. Every time something attracts me as a painter, whether it is a part of nature or some form of artwork, I begin to paint. I do this to find a way to let the beauty that has touched me find expression. Sometimes, it comes through the well of desire that is reaching for love. I try to develop images that focus my feelings as clearly as a mirror, and yet, there are times that love bewilders my expression. One fuels the other, and ultimately, I have to trust the heart to guide me. It is not within my human capabilities to sustain all the wonder and complexity of what is affecting me.

Creativity is so much more than just painting an image, writing a poem or making a song. It is finding expression for a love that is beyond form, beyond colors, beyond rules, beyond style, beyond identity, beyond everything. When we have finished, it is not uncommon to feel humbled and small in the exaltation of sharing in the power of creative freedom.

I feel every nuance of my perception, every beat of my heart, and I carry the longing to find expression for the wellspring of creativity rising up within me. Sometimes, I just put on the music, begin to paint, and am completely connected with my muse. My heart opens, and I look forward to meet what is coming through and appearing in my paintings. The excitement is in seeing the transformation that has taken place from what I envisioned to what has come through the actual images now before me. I watch to find out how the paint is appearing on the canvas, which often is much more interesting than I might have done if I had planned them.

Slowly, I fuse the forms and colors together in the fullness of the painting. The stream of feeling, the longing, the love, the shedding of the veils and the masks, the boldness to play, all come together, and I can feel how I am slowly learning to release control of it to become a part of creation in a birthing process. What is created will then act as a catalyst to stimulate the process in others when they see and feel and experience it as the viewer. It activates a greater receptivity to the spontaneity of life. I have seen it happen many times.

Artists are creatively seeking their own expression for the inexpressible, allowing the exotic blooms along the path to blossom. They become God-like, in union with the creative power, and the experience is so enlarged, so expanded, it has nothing to do with the smaller self. Artists are present to and within the creation totally, completely, in the fullness of the heart, soul and mind in a way that is surrendered to it as it flows through the body. The images that show up on the canvas or the sounds that are created through the music, mirror the feelings inside. The canvas and the medium disappear, and angels seem to shine through the creative freedom, and the light fills the heart to overflowing with the vintage wine of love.

POWER OF LIMITS

Don't look for water, become thirsty.
Necessity develops organs of perception!
O man, increase your necessity,
so that you may increase your perception.

RUMI

THERE ARE TIMES IN THE creative process when we are playing with ideas, and suddenly, we stumble upon an amazing inspiration. If this happens while we are short of resources and time, we often ignore it or set it aside for another time. In reality, we let go of it, no matter how exciting it seems at the moment of its conception. What we don't realize is that to proceed with the idea doesn't take unlimited resources outside of ourselves, it takes love and extended creative power. As Rumi describes, necessity provides an incentive, which is the mother of invention. Limitation sparks the flaring fire of inspiration.

If, instead of letting ideas diminish or disappear because of limited finance or minimal time, we embrace them creatively, we can capitalize on them by pursuing our creative flow. In this case, they would be viewed as an opportunity rather than a problem, and we would marvel at the brilliance that can evolve from limitation.

Life is all about working with limitations and constraints of one type or another. The soul is positioned in the limited form of the body. No one likes the idea of being restricted, yet limitation is the fertile ground in which the seeds of creativity sprout and grow. Without the challenge of limitation, there is no need for creating anything. Unless limits are experienced, one would never be pushed into seeing things in new ways, for there would be no motivating desire or incentive to try it.

When we are limited by circumstance, situation, or supply, we are forced to work around that obstacle in order to accomplish whatever it is that we want. Challenges, when approached positively, become helpful in getting our creative juices flowing and even inspire us by inviting us to think differently and more creatively about a particular issue we might be facing.

Limits help to make things visible to us. The moment we become aware of the limits of something, we begin to differentiate and recognize distinction. This is fundamental to the development of perception. A thirsty person walking in a desert might explore in every direction, before he finds a patch of cloud in the sky, which is a limit that guides him to find much needed water and vegetation.

To a creative person, limitations are not liabilities. They are opportunities to clarify key issues, to reach deeper and prioritize, and to discover new and fresh solutions. A person can work with a limitation, or against it. The shape and size of a canvas, and the viscosity of paint, are limits that actually help to free an artist. The tensile strength and wolf tones of violin strings or the egos of actors can be treated as stimulants that summon creative tension within a person so that they seek to express what they feel. Limits and the pain of emotional longing can help a person to reach for healing.

Sometimes, a weakness can become a source of creative expression. When a grain of sand makes its way into the deepest parts of an oyster, it is obviously a very uncomfortable and irritating intruder. If the oyster had hands and feet, it would have gotten rid of the sand immediately. Instead, it begins to cover the grain of sand with layer upon layer of its silky, defensive substance. Over years of steadfast struggle and great effort, the oyster creates an internal environment enriched by a lasting precious pearl. A beautiful unique pearl is developed through the limitation and discomfort of a painful and irritating invasion. The oyster and the pearl bring a new perspective to loving what we might have thought was our enemy. Rather than shutting down creativity, we can lay ourselves open to the stimulus of difficulties to discover something new that we might never have known was even possible.

When a person is forced to work within a strict framework, his imagination expands and reaches a peak, and it often produces some very rich ideas. In fact, when there is total freedom, the work is much more likely to fail. When Thomas Edison, one of the world's greatest inventors, was fourteen years old, he contracted scarlet fever. The fever, as well as an earlier blow to the head by an angry train conductor, caused him to become completely deaf in one ear and eighty percent deaf in the other. Instead of considering that as a weakness, he transformed it to work to his advantage.

On one occasion, Edison was called to help reduce noise levels associated with the elevated trains in New York City, which many specialists prior to him had failed to achieve. To pinpoint the exact location of the source of noise, he used his deafness to eliminate other distracting noises to locate the problem area. Within a short period of time, he discovered that the noise had to do with structural problems of the elevated tracks rather than the steam engines that ran the train as they first thought. While others could not hear beyond the sound of the engine, Edison was able to hear the cause of the problem due to his personal limits and constraints. Whatever happens to steal our freedom and truly challenge us to adjust, is often helping to open some new insight and perspective, if we pay attention to it, befriend it, and are willing to learn from it.

Freedom is not found in maximizing our inconsequential choices. Even though we may know this, we still battle with unnecessary and nonessential things in our creative life, as well as in our professional and personal life. Having no choice or option at all is certainly a painful burden, but having too many choices can also be painfully overwhelming and become an obstacle in the path of creative expression.

Maximizing petty choices is not freedom at all. The creative process requires us to have limited choices to develop momentum. A creative person needs to have boundaries in order to become liberated from them through the creative process of imagination. What seems confining, can become the path to true liberty through the power of creativity. Without boundaries, one would be like the old man in Frank Darabont's *Shawshank Redemption*, who had lived in the confinement of prison most of his life and when he was finally freed, he was desperately looking for the limits that would somehow protect him from the outside world.

On Sundays, I usually climb to the top of a mountain to watch the sunrise. Observing the natural elements as they develop various shapes is one of my most valuable inspirations. I am specifically intrigued by cloud formations and the variety of forms, figures and faces they create in the early morning. My fun is to stretch out my finger to move around and trace the edges of the clouds, as if I am painting and outlining the shapes in the air. My hand movement is creating forms that are familiar to me, while at the same time I am encountering forms that are visible outside of me. I feel the joy of seeing my dreams and fantasies becoming real. The patterns that are outside and beyond me are fusing with my perception. I am creating a movement that forms a kind of bridge between what is within me and what is outside of me. As the two patterns connect with each other, I experience a union between the outer images that I am seeing, with my muse.

From one side, I absorb and take into my heart what I am seeing and, from the other side, I align myself with the visual forms. This alignment becomes a kind of fusion that creates new forms with the uniqueness of their own. It is a way of balancing the different dimensions and uniting with the polarity they represent.

The process of creating begins with an outer attraction, a signal, a beckoning that triggers something within. Even if the person is not consciously aware of it, there is a subliminal response. We assimilate outer forms, and accommodate ourselves into them, from the inside to the outer form we see. There is an eternal dialogue that takes place between feeling and experiencing something, and creating it.

When I am painting and the paint suddenly runs down the canvas, I watch the shapes that it takes, and sometimes I am completely surprised by the images that I see forming around the dripping paint. In most cases, I capture one of the images and create around it, developing my own ways to capture the image.

Habits are formed through accommodating and assimilating what we encounter. How do we respond to it? To an artist, this response is a unique expression that can help develop their style. It is a bridge that develops between the artist and the creation. It is the very alchemy of transformation. When we allow this alchemy and become aware of it, we will be able to integrate it into our artistic expression.

Style is formed from the habits of the artist, the culture, the behavior, and choices. The medium of paint that an artist uses, the size and the shape of the canvas, and the make and quality of brushes, all become part of the limitations that the artist accommodates and utilizes to express their art. The limitations that might be considered an obstacle to an artist, actually help develop the potential to create. If we spend our time always wishing we had something different, we lose the opportunity to make something more of it.

While I was studying architecture, one of our class projects was to design a house without any limits. The land was flat, there were no setback requirements and the size of the house and the materials were all up to us. This assignment allowed us to discover how difficult it is to design without limitation. Through that I learned to welcome such limitations as safety codes, shape of the land, client's requirements and budget. I admit my best architectural designs have been those with the most constraints.

As artists, we adapt, we become flexible, we bend, and we make shifts toward the materials we have available to us, and we attempt to make the most that we can from them. We begin the process by allowing an interaction with what we have at hand. That is one of the ways we use limitation to bring freedom into our creative endeavors. When our perception is overshadowed by our current information or knowledge, we become restrained, because we see the physical forms and decide that the outer reality is just the way it appears. As a result, we give up our choice to see it in a new way, to assimilate it and respond to it in a creative way. The limits of forms that we are familiar with become the experiences of the artist. There is quite another reaction from the perspective of the one who is viewing it. The viewer has the same choice, to allow for something new to happen or not.

Often during the process of creation, something unexpected happens that interrupts the flow. Sometimes, noise from the outside becomes an intrusion, or perhaps someone calls on the phone. Any kind of interruption can change the flow of our intention. We can see that as limitation that prevents us from creating, or we can use it as a source of inspiration by really listening to the sound or feeling the energy of whoever is on the phone, and allowing it to flow into the creation in a new way. Suddenly, the experience is enlarged by what happens.

People expecting certain things from us can also seem like limitation. They may be quick to tell us what they think we should be creating, or we may be limited by how much time we have to create. All of these can be sources of anger and frustration, or they can become sources of inspiration. We are constantly making this kind of choice. We learn to draw encouragement from whatever we have to work with at the time. We respond with imagination, with a new way of seeing, that becomes part of the creation itself. We improvise and create with what we are given. The more we become aware of this process, the more we can affect what happens.

Many of the greatest works of art were created with cheap paints and materials that crack and form lines in the paintings. This can inspire us to choose our materials more carefully and helps define an artist's choices. These are limitations that become guidelines. Necessity can force us to create, because it pushes us into improvisation to use what we have in even better and more interesting ways.

If people could always go and purchase exactly what they want of the best there is to buy, no one would need to improvise, and everyone would simply become a consumer. No artists, scientists, inventors, or explorers would come out of such a society.

When I have had no canvas, I have painted on window shades. Sometimes I paint with the cheapest brushes that are offered in the market. Other times I use my fingers or a rag to paint with. All of these are means of achieving different effects in my paintings. As artists, we learn to turn limitation into improvisation. We could feel sorry for ourselves, not realizing that the very thing upsetting us, is giving us an opportunity to respond in a new way. If there is no limitation, there is very little to work with, except to make a copy of what we see. In many cases, we allow what has already been created to be the guide to the vision we try to reproduce, as in a still life.

What has been created can become even more attractive if it triggers a feeling deep within us. If an artist is hungry, he would see the fruit in a still life quite differently. It might become exaggerated, sensuous, and affected by the artist's desire for it. If what is created is unknown to us, then we accommodate it, and make it known by becoming familiar with it. That is the transition from the outer form to the inner feeling. The transformation of what we see into what we feel can produce great changes by the time we reflect something onto canvas.

When limitation triggers feelings, it emits an energy that can be turned into creative power. The shape of the instrument becomes the beauty of the sound that flows from it. The personality of the artist helps to create the images of the creation. The world is full of people complaining about the limitations and restrictions of their lives. These can become assets for an artist, whether it is an artist of life itself, a painter, a musician, a dancer, or a writer. What seem to be obstacles become the very assets for our creativity.

Our body has a certain way of moving. A knee only bends one way and an arm is restricted in certain movements. It may feel like a limitation in how we want to do certain things. What happens to that type of limitation if it becomes the very source of our power? The artist takes the form and accentuates it, glorifies it, and makes it noticeable. The limitation of our vocabulary allows us to create new words. The limitation of language allows artists to develop different ideas to capture what they want to express.

We bring feelings to the canvas, and we let them flow into shapes and forms and colors in ways that are totally unknown to a blank canvas. They may have been unknown to us until the moment we expressed them. We allow the feelings to guide the brush. A pianist allows the intensity of feelings to guide their fingers on the keys in an improvisation. If that does not happen, the pianist may be a very good technician at following the notes, but it becomes an outer event, not a creative flow between artist and piano.

Whatever we harbor in our subconscious affects what we express in some way. If we are a dancer, the length of our legs will affect the style of our dance. We don't think about it, and we don't plan what will happen. When we paint, we don't think and impose our thoughts on the canvas, we let the inner music of our feelings, the movement of spirit within us, flow into an expression that becomes a creation unique to the artist. As we expand this freedom, we develop a style that results from our own creative improvisation.

Inspiration is directly related to what we experience outwardly and to the way in which we take it into our inner world and respond to it. When the apple fell on Newton's head, he could have just sat there wondering why that kind of thing always happens to him, and he would have missed the creative reflection that led to the understanding of the great power of gravity, which affects everything that is done on earth.

An artist learns to lean into what seems to be a limitation and allows it to create a shift in the way the experience is perceived. Something new comes into being when that transformation is allowed, whether it is in relationship, in a life event, or in painting. Any limitation in form allows a greater freedom of spirit and soul, which is the precious gift of divine grace.

POWER OF NON-ATTACHMENT

Those who find delight in freedom from attachment

in the renunciation of clinging, free from the inflow of thoughts,

they are like shining lights,

having reached final liberation in the world.

BUDDHA

ATTACHMENT IS LIKE A TREE with strong roots that spreads across the garden of life and bears the fruit of anxiety, depression and worry. This tree draws its strength and is fed by a person's thoughts and belief that they do not have what is needed to be happy. It spreads like weeds when we are trying to achieve a certain goal, to possess someone, or to attain wealth. It also spreads when the attachment is to protecting the self from not having wealth, success, or happiness. Attachment can also be to deadlines, to stress, to a lack of time, as well as to sex, alcohol, food, and so on.

The tree of attachment is heavy with regret every time we are heartbroken over what we have lost in life, such as health, money, someone we loved, or our freedom. The tree develops strength when we are attached to the idea of being completely free from health problems, relationship issues, unhappiness, or other imaginary illusions that concern us even before they have happened.

Every time we become anxious, depressed, overloaded, or lose our peace of mind, we need to pay attention to the tree of attachment. We have to eliminate the burden of its fruits and flowers, and trim it as much as we can so the garden of life can have peace and love growing in its place. Even when we are attached to our creative power, and are not letting the power of creativity flow through us, we become susceptible to allowing burden, disappointment, worry and heartbreak to grow inside of us.

As human beings, we usually have some idea about who we are, the way we want to live, and we have opinions about what other people should be like, or how they should live. Our attachments to these ideas cause most of our suffering. It is our own concepts of reality, and not the reality itself, that make us experience pain. This is because what we believe affects how we see, perceive and experience. When we change our ideas about something, it also changes the way we feel about it.

A Tao practice for becoming enlightened is to spend hours meditating in order to be released from attachment to any idea. Meditation loosens the hold of attachment and helps us learn how to detach. It is a good practice for releasing stress that we feel throughout the day.

The best practice for me has been to become drowned in my painting to allow the creative flow to wash away any traumatic feelings. Usually, as I paint, my mind begins to wander and drift away from stressful thoughts. I soon find I am no longer attached to any thought or idea about what is stressful, boring, painful, interesting, entertaining, uncomfortable, or any other judgment I might have made about what is happening. One of the greatest things about the creative process is that it does not allow us to cling to any thought for too long.

In everyday life, there are regularly things that attract us, people who catch our attention, foods we like, and attractive things that we want to own or try to make part of our life in some way. Filling our lives with things we enjoy seems to be a natural pursuit. But, in truth, wanting to have things can be a path to pain as we try to protect and keep them out of the fear of losing what we have. The path to serenity allows the flow without holding on to anything or anyone too tightly. We appreciate and are grateful, but do not become attached to them.

The word 'attachment' is used widely in the mystical world to describe a person's relationship with the physical world and is often talked about as being the root of human pains and suffering. Mystics believe that the more one is attached to the corporal world the more they will suffer, so to be free of suffering, one must abandon all attachments.

Attachments come in various ways, for many different reasons and often arouse feelings of great intensity. They are almost always connected to the thoughts and expectations that we project on someone or something that we want to have. Whether we are attached to a job situation, a romantic relationship, an automobile, or the opinion of other people, we are directly connected to a thought we are holding onto that makes us cling to it. When a person is attached to money, for instance, they cling to certain ideas about their need for money and all the reasons why they *must have* money to be secure and happy.

We can become attached to something when we devote a great amount of time and energy to acquire it. Once we have it, we desperately try to hold on to it and keep it for ourselves out of fear we might lose it. As long as this desperate feeling exists within us, we can never have peace of mind. William Blake wrote:

> *He who binds to himself a joy*
> *Does the winged life destroy;*
> *But he who kisses the joy as it flies*
> *Lives in Eternity's sunrise.*

Imperative to the creative process is continuing to *leila*, to find the rhythm of creating and releasing, and to keep being open to whatever happens. When we *leila*, we emerge from nothing and remain in a state of non-attachment, which means we are allowing creation energy to flow through us. As we create, we simultaneously destroy or let go of something to make room for what is new. When an artist places a stroke of orange color over blue on his canvas, he is eliminating the blue, at the same time he is giving expression to orange. This brings a new appearance and a fresh look to the painting. Creation becomes possible when we learn to live open to each moment. This can only happen in a creative state of non-attachment.

While I am painting, as long as I don't envision or imagine the entire canvas, I am able to continue to play and experiment with the paint in a non-attached state of creation. I stay close to the canvas, so that I will not see the relationship between the various parts of the developing image in the beginning. The moment I step back and see the painting as a whole, I develop a connection between what I know and the aspects of reality that I discover on the canvas. This is what happens when I am involved with editing. As long as I am not attached to what I see, wanting it to turn out a certain way, I can eliminate everything quite easily, similar to a film editor.

When I move closer to the canvas, I face infinite possibilities of what it might become. When I step back, the possibilities immediately become more limited. This is how I distinguish the artist from the editor within myself. To the artist, there is no limit. This is the state when new ideas present themselves. To the editor, on the other hand, knowledge, technique and actions become important tools, very much like a designer who has to deal with limitations and constraints to adapt to what is needed for a design. The death of artistic achievement comes when the tools become the primary means of creating. The act of creation begins with attachments and limitations and strives toward the freedom of manifesting something completely new.

To *leila* and to be free of attachments, one needs to see everything as dispensable, whether it is a thought, an idea, a situation, or an object. Being ruthless is simply a part of the creative process and is important to the way we create, which is very similar to nature itself. That is the key to freedom from attachment. No matter how harsh, fatalistic or negative it may sound, in some way, one has to allow the ruins to be free to create something new.

One of the biggest challenges I have faced in my life was when I decided to give up my profession as an architect to become a painter. To let go of a successful and thriving career and become a starving artist was a decision no one in their rational mind would support. I had spent twelve years of my life developing what seemed like a successful life from the outside looking in. What I had not noticed during those years, was the continually accumulating attachments I was gathering around me until it became a large pile that I was smothered under. I had lost my freedom, and with it, my joy in creating.

When nothing is disposable, and everything seems to be fixed, one needs to be willing to let go of anything and everything. This is easily said, but how can one give away all the things they have gathered, end all the relationships of a profession, and willfully begin living in transience? To be willing to let go of all that we have or expect to have, and to approach the world with a general attitude of non-attachment, we need very strong internal motivation. How can a person willingly detach themselves from all the protections they have developed around them for security?

I had established a solid business, was designing exquisite homes, drawing an excellent income and seeing my designs published internationally, but inside I was unhappy. There was a war going on within me, and I was suffering because I could not let go of my attachment to this way of life.

Pressurized and entrapped by those conditions, I realized I had strayed too far and was failing to listen to my muse. I had to set the child within me free and guide him to a new creative playground where wealth, admiration, and all the physical assets would be meaningless. The first thing to do was give up the time I was spending watching television and trying to figure out what was going on in the socio-economic and political arenas of the world. I also needed to give up trying to listen to all the opinions of who was doing what and where in the architectural world. I needed to begin working on my own personal growth and develop some kind of spiritual practice. I began reading inspirational and motivational books and attending self-realization workshops.

All the things I was learning, were pointing toward one primary direction, which had to do with the process of letting go of my attachments in order to increase my internal happiness and sense of wellbeing. The principle was simple, but exactly what did it mean to let go, to not be attached to what I have? And, what would I have to do to get there? After several months of wallowing in confusion, I finally made up my mind to get out of architecture and follow the love of my life, which was painting, even though I had to start over as a starving artist.

On a cold winter night, I built up a fire in the back of my house and began burning every paper and design I had which related to my architectural practice. I began with my degree of architecture, and then I burned every file, document, contract, tax and insurance paper, every magazine that featured my designs until no paper was left that connected me with my past.

The very last thing I was attached to was an old photograph of my parents sitting next to each other, with me as a one year old sitting on my father's lap. It was an old black and white photo that I carried in my billfold as the only memory of my childhood with my parents. The picture had turned a sepia color and was cracked and had mostly faded from age. With tears rolling down my face, I finally placed the picture in the fire and put an end to all my attachments, including the memories. Once the outer aspects of my consciousness were gone, I was able to experience peace in the moment and find the freedom to begin again.

The spiritual cure for misery and anxiety is to learn not to be attached to the fruits or results of anything we do, even if they seem necessary or very important to us at the time. Non-attachment is being willing to allow whatever needs to happen to happen. To be free of the need for a certain result from any action is one of the secrets to enlightenment. When an action comes out of love, nothing will really be lost, and one stands to gain utmost peace and joy.

When I burned everything that had to do with my architectural practice, I became completely detached from what had been a major part of my life. This is not necessarily the only alternative I would recommend. A less drastic alternative is to develop an attitude of non-attachment by letting go of a way of living that imprisons us. This means making a subtle transformation from one lifestyle to another. My experience, although bold in execution, resulted in me giving eight years of unremitting love, trust and perseverance until I was able to make a reasonable living and recover my joy of creating through my new career as a painter.

Detachment is to be disconnected from everything external and to totally disregard what we thought we had to have to continue. Initially, it may seem to be a comfortable state to be in, but it is only a transitory stage between attachment and its alternative, which is non-attachment. The difference between the two is that detachment is static, while non-attachment is dynamic and changing. Detachment is a full withdrawal from things, while non-attachment can participate in everything, initiate movement and continue to be active and interested. The state needed for developing creative power is non-attachment. The defining aspect of it is found in love and inspiration, two extremely important elements in creativity.

My process of reaching detachment was to let go of all attachments, which can be uncaring and impose an emotional distance that can be upsetting to everyone involved. People usually fear this state, for if they were to let go of their attachments, the result would be to become unkind or inhumane to those involved, which is why non-attachment is a much more powerful choice in the creative process. It is inclusive and loving in its intention.

New ideas usually present themselves in a non-judgmental way when our awareness does not discriminate. In such a state, old ideas are released, and actions become important. This is the state when a person begins to see things appearing for the first time. During the creative process, the mind is like the beginner's mind, which is open to infinite possibilities.

The creative process is a quest. To take the journey, one has to be equipped with certain skills and knowledge that trusts and values intuition, and knows that creativity is much more than a coincidence or a lucky guess. It has to do with what Michelangelo called *intelleto*, that inner knowledge many do not know they possess. As the journey continues, there is a need to trust that the right way will reveal itself, and we become a witness to its unfolding. We move forward through the darkness with perseverance, looking for clues, following our perception to continue in ways we would not have discovered outside this process.

The process of creative expression calls us to rest and relax into our own experience of discovery as we explore in a territory that is new for us. We need to release the load we have carried around in the past. As we practice, we overcome the anxiety of not knowing where we are going, and we develop a capacity to tolerate the mystery, and ultimately, we find our way through the chaos. The creative space needs to be an open playground where the artist can enjoy the process of constantly discovering something new. The mind of the artist has to feel some stability as the process leads into the cloud of unknowing, as it can feel as if we are floating in an unfamiliar sky.

It is a powerfully liberating sacrifice, a strange kind of exhilaration, to love with all our hearts and to feel the ecstasy of spreading the wings of our souls, even if we fly in different directions, because we are not binding another to us through promises, through guilt, through obligation, or any other means of holding on to satisfy our own smaller needs and wants. It is a quality that gives to both, to let both taste the sweetness of freedom, which only happens when we are truly able to love deeply and still be true to ourselves and follow our hearts.

We call it divine love, pure love, and even sacrificial love, but it is the elevating generosity of loving another as we love ourselves. It is living freely and allowing true equality that lifts us into the beauty and wonder of having room enough to breathe and make the best possible choice for each and every heart. Non-attachment can become love's finest hour.

POWER OF CHAOS

Before the beginning of great brilliance, there must be chaos.
Before a brilliant person begins something great,
they must look foolish to the crowd.

I CHING

CREATIVITY IS AN ETERNAL HEALER, which is embedded in every person to treat any crisis that blocks the flow in life. As human beings we are all equipped with various tools of creativity that we can use when we respond to different cycles and different dimensions of our awareness. These tools are partly for construction and partly for destruction, so that we can receive replacements and repair works that need to be done for our growth and development.

Chaos is a divine mystery that exists beyond any kind of inner rhythm, order or rule in the creative process. In most English dictionaries, chaos is defined as *"the confused, unorganized state of primordial matter before the creation of distinct forms; the state of things in which chance is supreme."* So many creative ideas come to us in the strangest ways, often when they are least expected. Sometimes they seem to surface almost by accident. The accidental discovery is triggered by chaos and contradictions, rather than by order and logic.

Chaos is an essential part of the creative process. To be creative requires the embrace of confusion. New things don't happen when everything is perfect. Creativity is all about being out of order. The world is in constant chaos and so is life itself. As Nietzsche said, *"You must have chaos within you to give birth to a dancing star."*

There is the risk of ambiguity in the beginning of any new idea. Chaos is a part of the process, whether it is creating an artwork, a new business, or a new relationship. In the same way as it happens with plants, the sprouting seed rises up from out of the darkness, from the unknown and unpredictable, from the earth and from the body. The new order comes from the heart of the mystery outside our clever schemes.

Since there is no blueprint to follow, except for love and the desire to create, no one can claim that creativity is without pain. Many of the amazing opportunities that come to us for expanding on the material and spiritual levels evolve from complete disorder. The fewer choices we have to be anything other than ourselves, the fewer choices we have to do anything except what is meaningful to us. Discovering our true self, doing what matters, and becoming what we were born to be, is our mission in life.

People who work in creative fields often prefer a chaotic or disorderly environment around them while they work on new ideas or projects. The process of *leila* begins with the deconstruction of established patterns, in order to allow new ideas to arise from the chaos that has been left by the destruction. Creativity is a breakthrough, as a new and unexpected result rises from the wreckage of a former creative stumbling block. Even the simple act of making an omelet for breakfast, usually begins with breaking a few eggs, creating a new mix of things, and ends up leaving the chaos of several dirty dishes and containers behind.

Today, when we speak of chaos, we refer to a state of sheer confusion, of things or events, or both. The ancients did not separate chaos from creativity. In ancient religions, chaos was considered to be the first state of the universe, sometimes described as the emptiness of the outer darkness. This primal emptiness was the place where the creation of the universe could start.

Creative process operates somewhere between the ancient and modern definitions. In many areas chaos is a necessity for change. Artists see it as a portal to something unique, scientists are using it as a new way to describe certain forms or systems in nature, and business people ride the wave of chaos into exciting new patterns of commerce. In fact, using chaos in these fast moving times fosters the creativity necessary for success.

Chaos has the power to invite creativity, for it forces us to discover unique possibilities. It involves focusing on something in a new way, which brings about new associations that form unusual patterns. As the human mind is constantly seeking patterns in objects or happenings, it will take unrelated items and discover a pattern in them. By introducing random elements into a situation, new patterns and new ways of looking at a problem begin to emerge. Using chaos to allow these new patterns to form will lead to new directions in the creative flow within us as well as in our outer lives.

Chaos and the assembling of a new order are inseparable in the creative process. One without the other becomes uninteresting and fails to attract. Hollywood movies usually begin with a detailed development of a chaotic condition or the performance of a villain, who is the destroyer of some kind of order. After the audience is put in a fully frenzied state, the hero, or the good guy, appears to bring a new order to everything and relieve the audience from their frantic state of uneasiness. The more chaotic the initial conditions the more exciting the movie becomes.

While painting, I go through a similar process as the formula used in Hollywood movies. I begin a painting with a large brush or a piece of rag on a canvas that is primed black. The first colors I use are dark and I apply them to the canvas in a random manner, without trying to develop an order, until the whole surface of the canvas is covered with paint. I will then sit back and study the painting, looking for some means through which I can bring order and form to the painting. For me, the key to perceiving and recognizing some kind of a new order is to step back and see the entire painting in perspective. Once I find a form, I use lighter colors in an unfolding order to bring organization to the darkened state of the painting.

Artists usually distort or fragment features, or bring them together in an orderly manner to express a certain point or feeling. Here is when an artist gets in touch with those areas in themselves that are seeking expression. How do they see the world? How do they feel about what they paint? In what ways are they changing reality by the choices they make? What does the artist hope to share with others? What does their work reveal about their intention? What do the colors represent?

Nothing is predetermined in a work of art. The medium of art becomes a spontaneous union of the artist with the energy of creation that allows them to bring order to a series of random colors. In reality, there is no true chaos, just different levels of order, interlaced and folding in upon itself. Yehudi Menuhin, one of the greatest violinists of the 20th century, described how *"Music creates order out of chaos: for rhythm imposes unanimity upon the divergent, melody imposes continuity upon the disjointed, and harmony imposes compatibility upon the incongruous."*

What makes the world seem beautiful is the flow between order and the elements that bring it about. The eyes of the soul are the faculties for the creative action of spirit and flow of life. Everything seen through the eyes of the soul seeks an order that may better be described as harmony, because the eyes of love do not see anything as chaotic, and they do not bring negativity to the vision. Love stops the flow of negativity and transcends it, gives it wings, and opens the way to the enlightened vision of love that allows us to see a new and creative solution that we couldn't see before.

As long as a person remains surrendered to love, everything has a natural organizing harmony and balance. But, when love is pulling and drawing everything together on one side and reason is trying to interrupt and stop the movement because of fear or judgment about what will happen on the other, life becomes chaotic. This happens because there is a war going on between the two forces that exist within us.

When chaos is accepted as a part of creativity, the creative process receives a new order, which Sufis call *barakat*, meaning the assurance of receiving divine blessing. I think it is more than just blessing, because it is a repository in the soul, which is there whenever the soul seeks to flow in the movement of the creative energy. Such order comes to us to use it, certainly not to abuse it. If it is abused, chaotic challenges arise.

To make a living as an artist is very challenging, for we need to constantly adjust ourselves to the ups and downs of the ongoing economy. When the economic conditions are strong, most artists can draw sufficient income from the sales of their artworks, but when the market moves toward recession, sale of artwork drops. During a chaotic state of the economy, the first thing people cut back on is purchasing luxury items, and artworks are usually at the top of that list. When we are forced to use whatever we have wisely, we would buy food, seek the beauty of nature, and draw on the treasures of love and creativity to expand our wealth.

Just like the movements of the sea, there are times that the rising and falling waves of the economy move forward and there are times when they recede. Both times are valuable to an artist seeking balance through the creative process. During times of recession, we further develop our creativity, make proper shifts, and fill our stores with the abundance of new artworks. When the market begins to move upward, it is the time for promotion and sales. This is the way artists cope with economic turmoil, utilizing the chaotic states for bringing order and balance to their life, their art, and their career.

To bring order to a chaotic life, one has to go through the whole process of giving shape and uniqueness to ourselves. We learn to develop our own image. In a way, we paint ourselves into existence. The moment we freeze in the awareness that comes only through our external senses, we become like a stone. The ruby is still inside, but we become fixed, and the development stops.

When we are looking for order in chaos, we become an explorer, moving toward a discovery of the unknown, to meet and welcome the unborn, to remove the veil from the unseen, and to listen to what is unheard, to hear the silent cries of those who have no voice. Instead of thinking of getting rid of something that is wrong or negative, it is about surrendering to the faith and desire of loving. It is the recognition that there is *barakat*, a guiding love that is already there. That is how we are able to see the unseen. Our earthly eyes could not discern the invisible wealth we hold inside, for it is hidden from ordinary sight or from rational or mental solutions to the deeper challenges.

While sitting back and looking at my own paintings, the times that I enjoy the most are those when I begin to discover images that have appeared in the painting from the unknown. Those images have been flowing from one experience to the next without my concern about any order or arrangement. That is the raw and unvarnished play, which is not bound to follow any rules. It is the most fun of all creative activity. Such a play with raw material requires the freedom and faith in the creative process to prevent individual thinking from interfering with Michelangelo's *intelleto* or the divine intellect.

When we are in such a state, love uses all the perception in whatever way it is needed to create as a catalyst to nurture the expansion. It takes precedence over the rational caution and fear that holds us captive to rules. The flow of love silences the rational mind. It allows the brilliant light of divine intellect to develop and guide the process. It silences any attempt to place any rational restrictions to bring order to it. We allow the vision to develop a new perception that connects us with images of the past in a different way than when we are using our knowledge.

The full process of transformation cannot happen without chaos and confusion. Whether the change is a birth, a death, or falling in love, chaos is a pertinent part of the process. A seed in the ground struggles with much difficulty to rise above the surface, pushing through the dirt, rocks and resistance of solid ground. That is the first stage of challenge facing the plant, which is similar to the rising creative power that moves us through chaotic conditions. When the focus is on the positive aspects of confusion, the power of chaos becomes beneficial to creativity.

To be in the creative flow, one has to have a healthy acceptance of confusion, fear and anxiety, not as something to be avoided or run away from, but as the rich, fertile soil from which new ideas can sprout. Becoming a unique creative being is to let our personality develop without being affected by external or dominating influences, especially those dictating and imposing a morality that forces us into a corner. We need to be natural when we create, and to be a creative artist is a way to discover the pathway toward our own way of life. The uniqueness of an individual is what leads to transcendence, for it is not about being subjected and entrapped by the morals and virtues constructed and imposed by others.

It is the power implicit in chaos that allows for new discoveries and innovations. Somehow, chaos has to be experienced for a unique, harmonious order to develop and shine like light upon the darkness of turmoil and anguish. When we do this, we reach a new level of freedom, and we can confidently move forward to develop our own way of regulating that freedom. We become self-organizing. We continue to develop ourselves, and no one can challenge that direction once it becomes our experience. Ray Bradbury wrote, *"Every morning I jump out of bed and step on a landmine. The landmine is me. After the explosion, I spend the rest of the day putting the pieces together."*

The pieces we need to put together are what hold us back from freeing the flow. We have to loosen challenges that confront us. We need to break against the rocks of the fixed places in ourselves, and flow back out into the ocean of that which is greater than us to expand even further than we have been. When we experience creative power as the action and movement of chaos and order, what we create will express that truth.

We wander, search, long, pray, and we learn and travel, to scale the heights given to us, explore the depths, feel the pain, create boundaries, and let them dissolve again, and at some point, after what seems like endless yearning, something arises that brings order to our spirit. Some experience, some encounter and some presence makes itself known to us, and we become transformed by it. Everything that we thought we were washes into a transparent stream, a divine clarity that becomes a way of being, a way of seeing, and a way of feeling. A new way of living appears beyond our grasp or understanding, beyond our reaching, and beyond everything that we have known in the past and beyond everything that we are at that moment in time. The restless seeking stops. There is no more searching the outer manifestations of what has already been created.

This is a profound realization, and we are brought to a zero point in our existence, a standing still that calls us to create a new identity. We personalize it, because we are human and because we have borrowed a human form to harbor this inner awareness to walk in the world, to know the manifested reality that springs from the source of life, to somehow sense the divine center out of which it all flows. Can we know that which creates, apart from all that is created? It exists, whether we do or not, and yet, the magnetism that draws us ever more deeply into the unknowable, keeps expanding and drawing us into a deeper urge to coax something out of nothing, to attract the deepest stirrings in existence to show some kind of order or form to us. Love invites, pursues, and bewilders, lifting us to a peak where we can see a new vision through the eyes of love.

Volumes are created about what people have learned and felt during their encounters with the unknown. They have mapped the extraordinary, changing horizons within them, as they reached into the depths of the mystery and touched some small particle of it. They were empowered by encounters to reach beyond who they were and to feel more alive than ever before. Through paying attention, they discerned new directions to continue their quest. They learned to follow the lead of invisible energies that courted them and flowed through their dreams, playing with them, touching them, bewildering them, and coaxing them into expressing their beautiful inner experiences.

There are sacred moments when the blinding flash of light flames up from the union between the chaos and order. When we experience the eternal moment and a glimpse of the culmination of all searching, we somehow know with a mystifying certainty that it is for this moment that we were born. In an instant, we know the alpha and omega of life and our reason for being. In that instant, it is not about what we know in a cognitive sense, it is about what we are. We feel oneness with what is unknowable and know that we are made in the image of what cannot be known. Yet we are drawn to it, yearning for the unity with a beloved we have longed for all of our life.

In pure freedom, the universe is the clearest and most precious living being, filled with hearts and faces and forms of order that were all expressions of the love that reveals who we truly are in our wholeness. That recognition comes when nothing or no one is excluded, and all that has been, all that is, and all that will be becomes an ever growing, ever expanding, ever revealing mystical being that will forever enchant us with its revelations.

POWER OF MIND

The thought formed from delusion or logic
is not creative, for it evolves only from knowledge.
Logical thought belongs to skeptics.
The thought that guides the way of the wayfarer
is not from logic, but from the heart.

ATTAR

THROUGHOUT THIS BOOK, WE HAVE discussed the heart as the center and source of feelings and emotion as well as its power to generate creativity. We have described the power of the muse as the conductor of the creative process. We have also discussed how thought, rationality, memory, and opinion, which initiate from the mind, cause blockages in the creative flow. This chapter is about utilizing thought and rationality as a power to help rather than to halt the creative flow.

The mind is a storehouse of memories and the source through which experiences are interpreted. Most people tend to build their lives around what they think and believe. If they are searching to find ways to be free from pressure and pain, they try to eliminate it through the ideas and beliefs they hold. They seek to become educated and learn techniques of how to do things in order to avoid difficulties, and they develop a dependence on thinking their way out of their problems.

When thought is a mental or intellectual response, it deals with analyzing and evaluating what has been gathered as information. It cross-examines all the evidence, and uses reason to form a judgment based on the 'facts.' This kind of reasoning becomes the main process through which most people make choices and determine the direction of their lives. Mind is the primary source of human stability or security in this world.

To reach for a suitable solution to anything, we tend to allow the mind to use logic to deal with problems in a rational way according to our goals and plans. Rational thought needs the help of acquired knowledge to accept or reject what is reasonable or unreasonable, or what is probable or improbable. In such cases, thought helps to manipulate the information by mixing and matching concepts, ideas, and past experiences to allow a decision to be made. Here, we need the imaginative mind to spark new connections and fire the neurons that open new pathways and help us to consider creative options.

An imaginative mind is one that can visualize and explore beyond immediate reality and our understanding of it. This is a great ability that helps in developing the creative power and sustaining dreams with what we hope to create. Just as we master something by repeating it, we can do the same with our mind by visualizing it. The mind is not capable of recognizing the difference between actual doing and visualizing. This is what made Cubism such an influential movement in the twentieth century, when Braque and Picasso went beyond the known reality of the physical image of an object and expanded it into the imaginative multi-dimensional cubic forms that characterize their creations.

Many motivational speakers tell us that we can use this process to change negative habits and build new, positive habits or skills. They take it even further by saying that we can use the same process to attract money and possessions or for building a business, or to improve our health and relationships.

Our thoughts and imagination determine our failure or success. The satisfaction we experience in describing something can eliminate the desire to make it happen. If a person walks into my studio, sees the work in progress and asks me what it is that I am painting, my answer is usually, *"I don't know!"* If I describe what I'm going to paint, I am less likely to paint it. This is because my mind mistakes my talking about it for doing it and assumes that I have already painted that. A similar thing happens if I have planned to paint a particular subject or form. An artist friend of mine creates in a totally opposite way from the approach that I use! He feels when he describes his idea to someone, he makes a commitment to keep that vision, and that makes him work even harder to focus and manifest it on canvas. If he hadn't shared it with others, there is less chance of influencing what he paints by discussing it ahead of time.

The function of the mind, although it is the opposite of the function of the heart, is imperative in the creative process. Those who have allowed the heart and the mind to work together, have reached high levels of success, while the people who have placed them against each other, have missed the harmonious relationship that they could bring to the creative process. When the mind is envisioned as an enemy or a conflict, a reaction or struggle takes place against it, which can lead to a block in creativity. When the mind is set on serving and following the heart, it flourishes with imagination and the grace of love bringing harmony to life.

Before he started preschool, my son used to draw incredible and imaginative trees where one could see the tree from every angle. In the one drawing, we could see the tree from the top, from below, its every side as well as its roots. As soon as he began going to school, his trees began looking like lollipops, with a straight line as the trunk and a circle on the top as the branches and leaves. When I asked him what happened to the way he was drawing trees, he said this is how the teacher told him he should draw trees. From that time on, his free play became restricted to some kind of predetermined idea. Rational thinking had discouraged his imaginative mind, rather than allowing him to investigate possible ways to develop the uniqueness of his own vision.

It is important to recognize the difference between the conscious and the subconscious mind. The part of mind that deals with logic and reasoning is the conscious mind and the part that is responsible for all instinctive actions, such as heartbeat or breathing rate is the subconscious mind. Every day thoughts and beliefs develop in the subconscious mind like seeds which are continually sprouting, and they will eventually produce a crop or a fullness of vision. The conscious mind is like the gardener who chooses what to plant, but what develops in the inner garden, takes place subconsciously.

Our reality is fashioned when the conscious and subconscious work together. We can actually choose to set an intention in a positive way to guide the mind toward healing or restoring our wholeness. As an example, if in our breathing pattern, we decide to control the rate of our inhalation or exhalation, we would be using our conscious mind. As soon as we let go of controlling it and let it flow naturally, our subconscious mind takes the lead. Allowing the natural processes to work, gives us the kind of freedom that helps us to discover the joy in life.

Since thinking and believing manifest our reality, we can utilize power of mind by consciously developing positive ideas, emotions, thoughts and energy. This is how success or failure can become a conscious choice within our reach. When we bring our knowledge, our awareness, and our openness together, we connect our mind with our heart and the muse to bring longer lasting balance and happiness to our lives.

Thoughts have a powerful influence on us, and they can easily affect what happens to us. Unfortunately, most people neglect this important source of our human power and don't pay much attention to their thought processes, how their mind operates, what it is afraid of, what it focuses on, what it relates to itself and what it sets aside. Throughout the day, we do all kinds of activities paying minimal attention to how we are thinking at the time. The more we are aware of what affects our behavior, the more we are able to become a creative partner with it.

When I gave up architecture to become a painter, I was immediately faced with two major challenges. One was the rather poor economic conditions I lived in until I could achieve considerable recognition that would draw a proper income from my art. The other was having to live with the negative aspect of my own ego, which was in constant turmoil within me, as well as with those in my immediate surroundings.

To find a way to endure these serious conditions, I began to direct my thoughts toward the desired future of being a successful artist. I became watchful of funds and only spent money on what was absolutely needed. Every time I wanted something beyond my limited budget, I would tell myself if I gave it up in the present, I would have it for the future I envisioned. I utilized the imaginative aspects of my mind by making my thoughts work for me. I set the creative process in motion by guiding my thoughts to become a creative power working for my success, and I began to experience new opportunities.

I developed my ability to concentrate and control my thoughts, until it became part of my daily routine in everything I was doing. The process was difficult, but I did not think about or dwell on the difficulties, so I did not have to face them directly. I wrote *"I can do it"* everywhere around me, from my bathroom mirror to the refrigerator door, on my easel, car dashboard and everywhere else that was in my view during the day. Every time a negative thought would come to my mind, I would look at one of my *"I can do it"* notes, and did not let myself be carried away by negative thoughts. This helped to awaken all my abilities and powers, and to simultaneously replace the negative thoughts and self-doubt, which would have interfered with my goal.

At first, I was experiencing brief moments of peace, but slowly they lasted longer and brought me a new kind of power, an inner strength, a more compassionate love and kindness toward myself. I began to act from a different dimension of my ego, which was also connecting me more powerfully with my muse. People around me began sensing my strength and my paintings started to reveal this new direction by reflecting my new personality. My thoughts became soothing, healing and brought a confidence that showed in my work. When we consciously dispose of negative emotions and thoughts, positive thinking automatically becomes the dominating influence in our mind. As inner calmness develops, we become more compassionate in how we relate to others.

What we create is often the reflection of our mental condition. A person who is depressed is more likely to create works that reflect that depression, if he is truthful in his creative expression. The same is true of a cheerful person. If we try to change the outcome without having made adjustments to our internal thoughts and beliefs, it will only be a temporary, outer change and will prove to be futile in the end.

By training our conscious mind to think positively, with hopeful thoughts for success, while experiencing joy, appreciating our health, and enjoying prosperity, we eliminate the negative thoughts that cause us to fear, worry and doubt that we have the ability to be creative. When we do this, we are better able to tap into the source of our creativity. Life takes a much more positive turn when we keep our mind occupied with a hope for the best, and learn to control our thoughts to coincide with what we want in life. When we invite and are open to this positive energy, love becomes the muse and takes command of guiding our thoughts.

The same way that water takes the shape of its container, we create and manifest according to the images we hold in our mind. This is how the identity of an artist is formed and continues to develop. New directions in creativity come into existence through new thoughts. This is a journey of exploration. The secret is in concentrating, visualizing, observing details, having faith and projecting a new emotional energy into the mind by refueling and renewing. When the mind is cleared of negative thoughts, and only positive thoughts are allowed to guide it, the mind becomes a much greater influence and power, which can become instrumental in creating successfully.

Mastering creative power requires a balance between the mind, the heart and the muse. When the mind leads, we are able to expand our memory, improve our vision, and achieve the goals that affect our physical wellbeing. Since mind is capable of commanding and guiding the body, we allow the body to instinctively follow its command. When this instinctive control of the body is given to the mind's natural flow, we become free to follow our muse to create and allow the heart to bring us joy. This helps to form a harmony between these three elements so that they flow in one direction and work together with no need for counter balancing. When we have no fear of the flow being disrupted, there is no need to seek artificial measures or temporary solutions, our balance has been achieved.

By allowing the mind to manage the natural instincts of our bodily systems, we simply free them to do what they are meant to do. We are helping them to align with the energy that guides all creation. We are drawing creation energy through our bodies using our muse to call it forth. If the mind believes it can do something, it will find a way to do it, even when others think it is not possible. Once the mind is convinced, it takes control of the body and creates a passage for the muse, thereby allowing us to find our freedom from old ways of thinking that might be limiting us. When the mind and the heart unite, all organs of the body are in balance. When the body is in balance, the muse is allowed its greatest freedom. We remove the obstacles to make new connections, and we allow our uniqueness and creative energy to come through to express its power.

JUDGMENT AND CREATIVE POWER

To create is to bring about something new, to form values which simply did not exist before, to deliver and utilize old values in a new way, and to put together new combinations of values and ideas. When judgment clouds the creative process, it stops the flow, because it wants to relate to what has existed before and is familiar to us. At this point, the creative process comes to a halt. Judgment takes over, blocks our connection with the muse and pulls us away from the direction that would otherwise guide our creativity. We attempt to frantically pursue every direction that comes along and keep knocking at every door without discernment, for we feel we have lost the connection with who we thought we were.

Most of what we do in life deals with making a judgment of one kind or another. In the professional world, judgments and evaluations are made, and when the standard situations become identified and recognized, then the professional knows the probable course of the action to take, is aware of what might be a hindrance to it, and will turn to the standard means of handling the challenge. The task is to analyze the situation in order to identify the elements involved. This system works extremely well and is quite powerful. It is so effective that we have not seriously considered its limitations. Our standard for making a judgment may indeed be excellent, but it may not always be helpful in the creative process.

The creative process is about discovering our own path to freedom of expression. There are two different paths we can take, and we need to find our way between the two. There is a time when judgment and limitation take over, become dominant, and an obstruction is formed that steals our ability to relax. We are edgy and begin to find fault with things. Forms become entangled, confusing and block the opening of the door to creativity. We become weary, and we are not satisfied with anything. When we do this, we lose our creative ability. This is when we need to set aside our rational thinking and listen and watch and discover what the attraction is that is naturally pulling and drawing us toward creative expression. Freedom comes when the muse wants to play and dance with the possibilities in life. The opposite of *leila*, or 'free play' is to try and fit the solutions into a standard or generic form out of habit.

Creativity is a self-regulating power. When we create, we want to continue creating, and if we don't find a way to do that, we begin to lose the urge and desire. Creativity is a divine spark, and we fan that spark into a flame by playing and opening our imagination to possibility. The creative act itself has an energy that self organizes. It fuses things, and it does not separate them. It makes use of everything, whether in the light, or in the dark. It discovers the place where things seem to belong.

While we are creating, if we face the question of what to do next, we are inviting our judgment to take the reins. Having to ask what to do next, means one is in the logical mind rather than the creative flow. When someone asks me to look at their work and tell them what to do next, my answer is almost always the same. I tell them to wash their brushes and clean up, because they are done. In creativity, we allow the muse to move that process forward, and then we learn to *intuit* when to stop. We choose visualization as an appealing symbol or metaphor to guide us. It has been said that however we make love is how we create. How inventive are we? How free are we? How willing are we to try something different? We dare not lose our wildness, or we will put ourselves to sleep.

While Michelangelo was painting the ceiling of the Sistine Chapel, the pope kept asking him when the painting would be finished, and his answer was always the same, he told him it would be finished when it is finished. *Intelleto*, our divine intellect, guides the process, not the individual mind. Creative process cannot be tied to any time frame, to any product or used to achieve a predetermined end result. We let the creative power lift us into the energy of whatever vision is expressing through us, and we learn to work with it, not against it.

Being on a path that will bring excitement and joy to our lives activates creative power. We know we are on this path when the feeling is activated in our hearts by igniting the spark of love. We feel it stirring and touching the center where love begins to move us and give meaning to our life. When something touches that center, it melts the frost from our bodies, helps us discover our vulnerability and moves us to experience the power of feeling!

Judgment about what we have already created only has value after the work is done. Artists have generally been successful in creating frameworks of judgment through which their work can be appreciated. Whenever a new movement is introduced in the arts, the work cannot be appreciated or evaluated through the old standards. Once new guidelines are established by the critics, what was once considered unacceptable suddenly finds value and significance, and becomes a new trend or style in art. Many examples of this can be found throughout history, such as in the development of Impressionism and Cubism. There are a few other disciplines, such as architecture, where the creators define the standards through which the artwork is to be judged and valued.

In today's art world, a work that expresses the value of logic is usually not seen as creative, while an idea which is simply unique or unusual tends to be perceived quite differently. This attitude sometimes has a negative impact on creativity, because those who wish to be considered creative come up with bizarre ideas instead of those which help us visualize in a new way. This causes the public to see creativity as a marginal luxury rather than an important or necessary part of life. I have a friend who is not very creative, but he wears strange clothes and wears his hair in a peculiar style, as if he wants to be seen as an artistic figure by giving an impression of originality and non-conformity.

When we respond to the creative process, our judgment comes in two ways, either through a constructive response or as a response that obstructs our freedom to express. Constructive judgment is feedback that we receive while creating, and it generally becomes a facilitator for any further action. Judgment that obstructs our originality shows up as a challenger, stepping in either before or after we have created something. When it comes in before the forms have shown up, it can become a block to creativity, which would freeze our creative flow. If the judgment comes after we have created, it may bring rejection or indifference. The challenge for us is to recognize the difference and to cultivate a more constructive response accordingly. From that time on, we *leila* between ongoing creative work and becoming more positive in our evaluation of what we create. One is the muse and the other is the editor. The two begin to flow together like dancing partners – the muse leads and the editor follows. When the two are synchronized in such a way that they become difficult to tell apart, we have actualized and enabled our ability to use the power of the mind to help us develop the creative process.

By befriending both the muse and the editor, we help to free them to work together, allowing one to enhance the other. The fusion process is at work within us in subtle ways at the same time as it is developing our artistic vision and creativity. It is a way of befriending and developing the amazing, perceptual insight that already exists within us.

POWER OF BLOCK BUSTING

What I try to do is write. I may write for two weeks 'the cat sat on the mat, that is that, not a rat.' And it might be just the most boring and awful stuff. But I try. When I'm writing, I write. And then it's as if the muse is convinced that I'm serious and says, 'Okay. Okay. I'll come.'

MAYA ANGELOU

THE FLOW OF CREATIVITY TAKES place through what we take in as well as what we put out. If it is only about one of the two, the movement comes to a halt. We learn techniques in order to let go of them and find our own. One of the ways this is done is through submitting what we learn to the unseen presence of the muse in our subconscious. We intuit, we perceive, or we simply have faith in what is dwelling within us in order to move toward the unknown. We learn about whatever attracts us, and proceed to develop our ability to express it. The process is initiated by our taking a step forward and doing something. The Red Sea does not part until Moses takes a step of faith to call for the water to move.

What takes place in the process is a union between the limitation of judgment and technical ability on the one hand, and the freedom that flows within to take us beyond limitation. This flow swings back and forth, up and down, and in a spiraling movement like the whirling cloud of light that surrounded Moses. It is the way of the muse, as it expands, gives, and breathes out, and the way of the monitor or editor as it contracts, receives and breathes in. One minute we are making, and the next we are eliminating what is unnecessary to what we are creating. In the imaginary realm, we are making love, and move away from love in order to be able to return to it. This is the power that busts, melts, dissolves, burns, destroys, and reduces whatever could block creative flow.

The process of creativity begins with a conscious action of stepping forward, and allowing the muse to guide as we surrender to the creative flow. When I feel good, I usually paint, and conversely, whenever I paint I'm led into feeling good. My rhythmic creative process of *leila* becomes more fun when I forget about what I am doing and playfully explore the possibilities. When creativity has to do with making money, or about becoming successful, or about winning, it ceases to offer that same kind of exhilaration and excitement. When we become acutely aware that we are no longer having fun, we lose our incentive and consequently, we also lose the joyful feeling that comes from creating.

It is surrender that allows the thoughts of the mind to fall into the realm of the subconscious, helping us to release whatever is blocking the flow and move toward the unknown. It is true that certain skills need to be developed in order to express emotions in a creative way, but learning something new is not the only medium or way to do this. Skills are mostly developed through practice, until one reaches a point of being able to do things without thinking, much in the same way that fingers learn to respond to the visual cues when typing. With practice, we don't have to stop and consciously think about where each letter is as we type.

An artist friend of mine paints while he is listening to regular programs on commercial radio stations. This includes music, advertising, talking, and all other typical sounds of programming. I cannot imagine how he is able to do that. For me, that would be very confusing. I do listen to music, especially improvised music, which inspires me and moves me away from letting my mind control my expression and also helps me relax into the rhythm of my muse. When I discussed it with my friend, he told me that the constant noise was a buffer against all his thoughts, and allowed him to paint from a deeper source while his mind is engaged in other things. The technique is hidden in his subconscious, and it works to help him stay focused. We each have to find the process that helps us discover how to connect with the muse so we can be free to express creatively from that source of energy.

We develop technique in the physical realm in order to find the best ways to express creative thoughts and ideas. It expands our capability, and once filled with a technique, it flows easily through the medium of expression we choose. This is quite different from the times when it spontaneously breaks through us, free and unplanned, like a bird flying out of the nest. That freedom is not the same as the rational movement that has conscious intention, yet it is guided by instinct and seems to have a momentum of its own.

It is important to recognize the difference between making and creating. A person faces the difficulties and does the hard work necessary in order to make or construct some kind of finished product that satisfies them or someone else. Creativity is distinguished by the freedom that brings such enjoyment while one is in the creative flow. It is the process that is so energizing, because the end result is not a conscious focus.

Everyone has some kind of a dream. There are those who just enjoy dreaming and those who move their dreams into reality to bring them into an expression. To manifest a dream, knowledge and capability come together through the energy of love and by following the muse. The more one knows and trusts the guiding power of the muse, the more rewarding the result will be. At its best, it is the mastery of balance coupled with surrender that has brought about the greats who have created so much for humanity.

Mastering the creative process is not about doing things in 'a perfect way.' When a person describes himself as a perfectionist, he is simply trying to develop his skills through an expectation of what will make them perfect. Imagine what would happen if the person moves in the opposite direction, which is to see what develops rather than trying to control its development! Creativity is like being in a kind of wonderland, where one is longing to realize and taste the fullness of beauty in everything they encounter. In most cases it is not pursuing perfection nor settling for less, which yields the true creative surprise.

I often hear from my students and friends that they have moved away from creating for a while, and they begin to worry that they have lost the power of creativity. How could this happen? Everyone experiences periods of not creating, and it is valuable to take a break to renew and develop new perspective. Otherwise, one would fall into repetition and the pursuit of what is familiar. The movement of variation and the exploration of different directions is needed to come face to face with a person's capacity to create. If we feel we can't do something, it becomes difficult to move forward. We lose velocity. Sometimes, when an artist stops creating, they don't just stop, they begin to stagnate. This is what is called writer's block or better yet, a creativity block.

It is obviously a devastating feeling for an artist to feel the loss of inspiration and to be encountering blocks. It is important to know that creative power will never be abolished or lost completely. Creative block is similar to a dam that blocks the flow of a river. Just as water accumulates behind a dam, creative juices pool behind a block in the same way. Suffering from creative block does not mean we have lost our artistic ability. It is important for us to know that it can be overcome.

Creativity blocks have many causes. A serious kind of blockage may happen as a result of difficult circumstances in our life, such as physical illness, depression, the breakup of a relationship, or financial pressures. Other times, it may have to do with demands of our career, such as being compelled to produce works that are against our natural inclination and rhythm. Too much pressure causes stress. We may be pushed to move too fast or be forced to work in some style or genre that is unsuitable for our abilities.

Sometimes other people, like our school teachers, friends and relatives or even a complete stranger may feel that what we have created is ridiculous enough to make remarks that cause us to freeze and lose the incentive to create. We are taught to follow the rules, be logical and not deviate from standards, so that we might stay on the straight, narrow and socially-acceptable career path. Most of the time this is useful, but when it comes to creativity, it is bothersome and can drain our energy coming to terms with it.

Unfortunately, the competitive and judgmental nature of human beings habitually lead to the evaluation of others and their ideas, even when we are consciously aware of the negative effect it will have on them. That is why, during my creativity retreats, everyone learns that *no judgment* is a very basic rule in creative play. There is no doubt that our environment can be supportive and nurturing as well as being obstructive to living a creative way of life. We can deliberately build an environment that is full of creative stimuli, or one that is very comforting and peaceful. Effective creative environments can vary with people and their moods, so everyone needs to experiment with their surroundings in a way that will help to build the most effective and supportive environment.

The creative process is at its best when it is in the overflowing mode, which happens after we have been non-productive for a period of time because of experiencing some block. The overflow usually takes us in an unexpected direction that is new, even in our own creative course, especially if we have spent our non-creative time doing positive things. Some of the positive things I do during this period away from painting are to study the works and lives of other artists, visit galleries and surf the internet to see what other people are doing.

Other positive things I do when I am not actually producing art, is to increase my promotional and marketing activities. I send postcards and flyers to my collectors and galleries, research upcoming art fairs or events where I could possibly exhibit my art. I update my websites, online portfolios, my artist's statements, and I may have some leaflets or brochures printed up about myself and my latest works.

The most serious block that obstructs all creative flow is fear, especially the fear of failure. We are afraid that what we create is not going to be good enough, so we give up, because we think we cannot live up to it. Only when we accept that not everything we create is going to be, nor should it be perfect, can we liberate ourselves from the block. I have completed paintings that I have not released, because I don't think they are good enough. The funny thing is that, sometimes, what I think is bad, turns out to be a very significant and well-received work. By focusing on the process instead of the product we can avoid getting caught up in the quest for perfection.

Being overwhelmed by the creative works of other artists, or by the great masters, can also trigger a block. In cases like that, we compare ourselves with those whose work we appreciate and admire. As a result, we begin to deviate from our true self and feel we can never reach their level of mastery. It took Brahms twenty two years to finish his first symphony, because he was such an admirer of Beethoven's symphonies, and he persisted in comparing them with his own compositions. Ideas of perfectionism made Brahms compare his work with Beethoven, and since he thought he could not possibly measure up, he put off writing his symphony for a very long time.

Another cause of blocks can be the fear of feeling ashamed, or making a fool out of ourselves. This often happens during my seminars when a person feels that he or she did not grasp what I was discussing, but they feel too ashamed to speak out, until someone else asks a question. Then they speak up, admitting, *"I thought I was the only one who felt that way."*

When creative block happens to me, I know that it is temporary, and that prevents me from getting nervous or anxious about it. There are times that I cannot stand the sight of my paintings, and I think I will never paint again, but shortly after the initial reaction, I find myself holding a brush in hand and having a great time playing and *leilaing* with colors and forms.

Through years of painting, I have found several methods that help me restore my creativity levels at will. The very first thing I do is to refuse to worry a bit about it. If worse comes to worst, and I don't seem to be able to produce any painting, I simply regard the time as a period of artistic hibernation. I know and have faith that my muse will rise again, and it will take me to a higher level of creativity as it always has before.

To remove creativity blocks and encourage my muse to rise again, I have a ritual of organizing my environment. I clean up my palette, wash the brushes, move them around in a new arrangement, and I dust around my studio. This ritual is meditative and prepares me to make a shift, to move into a rhythm with my awakening muse. In sacred ceremonial rituals, we become mindless, and we move into a feeling of inspiration and faith. We learn how we benefit from the rituals, and we also learn how we lose them, yielding the practices to discover we still have the pattern of the rhythm within us. As we develop our own rituals and practices, we become freer to follow our own direction.

Creative blocks can happen at any phase of creative flow, even in the life of fully developed writers, musicians and artists, but it most often happens in the earlier stages of creativity. It occurs when we have somehow discovered and recognized our creativity, and we hear friends and relatives admiring our works, when our skills are still not fully developed, yet we have already begun to think of ourselves as artists. In such cases, obstructive judgment runs perpendicular to the line of action, interposing itself even before we begin to create.

When the mind is running fresh on inspiration, and is uncluttered, creativity keeps on flowing. But when our mind is filled with judgments of our own creations, we enter a dangerous stage where we become extremely disappointed if we create anything less than what we would consider a masterpiece. Our creativity usually falls short of our expectation, and thinking of new ideas and concepts becomes very difficult. We have developed the pain of what I call creative constipation. The symptoms are the drying up of our creative juices and the uneasy conditions of confusion and psychological disparity.

An important factor to comprehend in the creative process is that we shall not like or dislike our creation for more than a moment. If we did, we would face the problems of comparison. The creative process offers us joy and exuberance, and it is not about what is produced by it. The moment our mind notices the product, we ask ourselves if it is good enough. If our answer is positive, sooner or later we have to perform again and our judging voice reminds us that this creation should be even better than the last one. This is when we freeze up, because we are competing against ourselves, dealing with our own ideas of success and failure.

The most destructive source of blocks to our creativity hides within us. It is our subconscious and that little voice inside our mind that we call ego, which warns us of the dangers of unconventional ideas. Although people and things around us can make it harder or easier to get into the creative flow, in the final analysis, all blocks are internal and are caused by the ego. Since this issue is so vital in the course of creativity, we will discuss it in more detail in the following chapter on the power of the ego.

Total freedom to create comes when we develop a belief that anything we construct or build ends up in destruction. When some artists tell me they are blocked, I instruct them to paint several canvases with the intention of burning them. They are shocked at the beginning and argue with me to be less ruthless. When they recognize my persistence, they realize there must be something valuable in this action. The moment they begin to paint to burn, suddenly they are relieved from their blocks and back in the creative flow. What happens in this action is the development of a love for what they are doing and the elimination of any attachment to the result since they are going to throw it away. Love is needed for them to move forward to discover the next level of creativity.

As a man from the Middle East, I grew up in a culture that was oppressive to women. Since many of them were veiled, I began to imagine and connect with their inner beauty. This ultimately became a guide in both my life and my art. It was the mystery of what was unseen that attracted me, and I began to express something deeper than the outer appearance. I was venturing into an unknown, and it guided me on an inward journey that stirred my heart and awakened my muse. I began to paint the revelations of the heart. I was reaching to paint the mysterious glow of a radiant energy that became a metaphor for love, for truth, for light, and for life itself. It is a vision that connects me with the longings of those who view and respond to my art.

When we connect with our dream, we indulge ourselves in visions of bigger pictures and escape from the mire of self-doubt and the challenges that could cause blockage by asking ourselves, what's the purpose of it all? What am I working towards? What is my unique mission to carry out? It is only when we have no attachment to the end result that we can spend a few quiet moments reflecting on our bigger creative dream. As we are creating, we find out we are subconsciously expressing our emotions through images, words, or music and we look back on them later as a way to reconnect with our muse.

Connecting with our muse, which is the part of us that is naturally exuberant, joyful, and free in its pure expression of creative thought, becomes our motivation to *leila*. We learn to listen for its wisdom and carry out its wishes.

This is how we can connect with our thoughts and learn what our ego, or inner critic, wants and how to peacefully coexist with it. We become aware that we have the power to change our perception, to out-think our fears and silence our inner critic, which could cause our blocks. When we don't have the fear of being rejected or the fear of financial insecurity, which might keep us from buying something wonderful that would inspire us creatively, we can move confidently toward our dreams. If we are without the fear of failure, we feel free to explore something new. Blockbusting is a tremendous energy saving process! What better way for us to protect and conserve energy, than to protect the valuable resources of our own creative power!

POWER OF EGO

When you paint, you forget everything except your object.
When you are too much engrossed in it, you are lost in it.
And when you are lost in it, your ego diminishes.
And when the ego diminishes, love infinite appears.

MEHR BABA

THE EGO IS A SMALL voice inside the brain that is associated with personal identity. It promotes and motivates us toward satisfying the self. It plays a very important role in the development of our lives, especially in our creative life.

The ego comprises the organized part of personality that includes defensive, perceptual, cognitive, and decision-making functions. Conscious awareness resides in the ego, although not all of the operations of the ego are conscious. The ego separates what is real from unreal, and it helps to organize and make sense of our thoughts in relation to the world around us.

The word ego is taken from Latin, which translates as "I myself" to express emphasis. The Latin term ego is used in English to translate "the I." In modern English, ego has several meanings. It could mean an individual's self-esteem, an inflated sense of self-worth, or in philosophical terms, one's self. However, according to Sigmund Freud, the ego is the part of the mind that contains our consciousness.

The Sufis call it *Nafs*, which is within everyone, and it is all about the self. *Nafs* or ego has no capability to love, but it can and does experience need, which is often easy to mistake for love. It can certainly love how another person makes us feel. Many Sufi practices are aimed at subduing or taming *Nafs*.

Although ego can be very helpful in developing the special identity in a creative person, true creativity and love do not come from it. Ego is equipped with a strong weapon called fear. No matter what the external circumstances of life, fear is internally fed, imposed by one part of ourselves onto another.

The main concern of the ego is with safety and allowing some of the desires of the self to be expressed, but only when the consequences of these actions are marginal. It also helps make us aware of our needs and wants us to experience the gratification of our deeds.

There are two distinguishing aspects of ego: positive or 'true ego' and negative or 'false ego.' Positive ego enables a person to feel like an individual human being, distinct from the mass and group identification. This is the aspect of the ego which is essential for creativity because only through the acknowledgment of 'I' as an individual can a person develop identity as a creative being. The negative aspect of ego is the one that deals with greed and fears of losing control. Negative ego likes to compete and to be better than anyone else for the purpose of self-exaggeration. It always wants to express that, *"I am the best, I am the most creative, and no one is better than me."*

Everyone has the capability to create his or her life exactly as they want it to be, full of joy, love, success and abundance. The opportunities are there for anyone who truly wants it and goes after it, but most people keep turning their backs on something new. Day after day we choose to do things that keep us away from living our dreams, and when we face unhappiness and misfortune, we blame the world around us for having created our problems, but the truth is that the source of all our suffering comes from developing a negative ego.

The negative ego is the limited, separated, illusory self which cannot see beyond its own limitation. It is the internal saboteur and our worst enemy that imprisons us in the dungeon and limits of the mind. It not only wants to control our life, it summons us to try to control other people's lives as well. There is a story of a rich man who starts having an unbearable pain in both his eyes. He visits every capable medical doctor all over the world for a cure, but no one is able to come up with a remedy for his pain.

This goes on until one day he learns about a holy man who lives in the Himalayas and performs miracles. Although he does not believe in miracles, he takes the chance and journeys to see the holy man. After he explains his pain, the holy man tells him that his eye problem is due to the fact that he sees too many colors and his cure is in seeing only green colors. Not having found any other remedy, the man orders all walls of his mansion to be painted green. After the job is done, he notices his pain is reducing. Excited about the result, he gives orders to have everything around him to be green to the point that even servants were to wear green and had to paint their faces and bodies green. Finally, he was seeing nothing but green and the pain had completely gone.

In order to show his appreciation, he arranged a great feast for the holy man and sent an escort to bring him into his mansion. Upon his arrival, the holy man walked around the place and kept on saying, *"Wow, everything is green."* The rich man showed his gratitude by thanking the holy man and told him how he appreciated his prescription. The holy man looked at him and said, *"You did not have to make the whole world around you green; all you had to do was to wear green glasses."*

There are so many times in life when our negative ego wants to change the whole world around us and prevent the muse from creating new ways for perceiving things.

What we don't realize is that the negative ego is not us, it is something we inadvertently created, and we never intended it to control our life or other people's lives. Most of the problems we face in life emerge from the negative ego, which is allowed to steal our power when we believe it is a real force outside us. It is the cause of all negative emotions, thoughts, behaviors, physical and psychological problems, relationship difficulties, poverty consciousness, lack of money, or whatever we could name that is ruining our lives. It is the negative ego that blocks the creative flow. In truth the negative ego could be defined as what causes an imbalanced life.

The positive ego, on the other hand, shows us what is happening in the outside world. Without it, we would not have any conscious awareness. As long as we live in our physical body, we need to have the balancing strength of a positive ego. The problem is that we habitually cannot see or recognize the positive purpose of ego to tell it apart from the negative purpose and often fail to discern the difference between the two. We say we love a certain food, or we love to sleep late, or we love to be admired, and yet, this has very little to do with what love is, more to do with what we want.

The essence of negative ego is fear, separation, and self-centeredness. The interesting thing is that the negative ego does not really have an existence by itself. Everyone has been created with a positive ego, but the moment we give in to the negative thoughts and ideas within the mind, we begin to live in that state of consciousness even though it is not our true nature. The reason is that we are living in a dream of the negative ego's interpretation of life, rather than interpreting life from the truth of the positive mind. There are ways to create a life that could allow us to live our inner peace, joy, peace of mind, love and happiness all the time regardless of what is going on around us, and there is the opposite way of choosing a life that could make us angry, upset, impatient, unstable, depressed, and sad.

When it comes to creating, the negative ego is attached to something 'out there,' which is actually a false illusion that something outside of the self is what makes a person happy. The power and strength of the positive ego is able to use whatever comes into life as a way to help make a change for the better. Sometimes, an outward event can help us to create joy and set us free from endlessly wanting someone else to provide our means of happiness. Taking responsibility for our own choices is challenging, but it helps us to step up and become the creator of our own existence.

No matter how much we remain true to our vision and how assured we are about our work, there might be people who will be critical of us for their own reasons. We can do nothing about that except to remain unyielding to our center and true to the guidance of our muse supported by the strength of our positive ego. It takes strength and courage, but as we learn to trust our muse, we will be more capable of facing the challenges that come our way, whether they are from the outer world or our inner persona. Regardless of any type of judgment, we need to feel good about ourselves and our work, and to not worry about what others might think or say.

Early in my artistic career, I had a typical experience that many emerging artists have, which is finding a gallery to exhibit and sell my art. I put together a nice portfolio of my paintings and started a tour of Los Angeles art galleries, in search of finding one that would accept my art. One gallery after another refused me, saying that my works were good, but not the type they usually exhibit. Although, being rejected was disappointing, one gallery owner made me furious by telling me that I had to take some painting classes and suggested I sign up with their painting classes for a weekly course for one year. For me, this was the straw that broke the camel's back.

My ego was badly hurt. After painting all my life and having studied fine arts, I was told I had to take lessons in painting! I was so upset that I stopped looking for galleries and began to think I should give up painting completely. My ego was making me feel constricted, painful, obsessed and severely disempowered. My energy level became low, and I could not take my mind away from my anxiety and pain. I was fighting with myself, trying to convince my ego that the gallery owner did not really mean that my art was that bad – perhaps he only wanted to promote his own art classes. No matter how much I tried, my ego kept coming back at me again and again, projecting doubt, anxiety and giving me an inferiority complex.

This condition went on for several months, and then something happened that changed my perspective. In a moment of unusual lucidity, I saw the future before my eyes. To eliminate my ego-driven pain, I had to follow the love of my heart. I had to paint and forget about wanting to show it to anyone for approval. This released me from becoming a victim of my negative ego, and it opened the possibility of making a different choice. I was able to rise beyond the negative thoughts into feeling empowered by love and the muse that encouraged my creative expression.

As I began creating for my own joy, I was not concerned about how another person saw my art. My painting was not something I did for others to see, and I was no longer painting with the idea of seeking their evaluation or judgment. Without being dependent on the opinion of others, I realized how much easier it was to be authentic and true to my own heart. I found a new approach, and it gave me the courage to refuse to be a slave to my own ego. I felt an inner freedom, and I was released from the belief that it was my outer life that made me happy. I was able to easily accept other people's opinions and viewpoints even when they were quite different from my own. I was able to do this because I began to dwell in the 'Now' – to live in the present moment. I became much more positive, creatively expressive and with this new direction, I felt the growth and expansion of my perception and personal vision.

My positive ego was like a spring that soothed me with feelings of serenity, and I developed a more peaceful outlook that gave me a sense of wellbeing and clarity. It was an inner assurance, an integrity that gave me more compassion for others. I was able to explore new approaches for being more creative in my art as well as in my life and relationships. I discovered that I would never truly be able to manifest anything meaningful in my life if I did not find a way to claim the right to my own personal creative power.

Living a joy-filled, creative life has a great deal to do with how creatively we are guided in the choices we make. Whether we name it the muse, or call it love, or speak of being guided by the heart, we become more aware of the influence of positive inner guidance. Are we listening to the voice that unites us with what is inspiring, or the negative voice that causes us to separate from our own inner power? Are we listening to the voice of love or the voice of fear? Are we listening to the negative voice of self-centeredness that entraps us in limitation where we believe we have no choice, or the voice of a universal consciousness of unlimited possibilities? The enlightened choice comes like the dawn, bringing insight and a new light of understanding to our own behavior. We are much more capable of taking responsibility for our actions.

Creativity comes forth from a relatively imaginative exploration of potentials that exist outside as well as inside of us. Then suddenly, a little voice inside the head appears and starts to challenge the creative muse that seeks our joy. It wants to dictate ideas and concepts about 'how things should be.' The result is a condition of the negative ego that allows rational thought to take over our awareness by trying to control and limit how we create.

When people either seriously or jokingly say, "*The devil made me do it*," they are projecting the blame outside of themselves for something that has happened instead of taking the responsibility for it. The negative ego could easily be personified as that nasty, little guy that sits on our shoulder convincing us to do unfortunate things. The positive ego is the little angel that sits on the other shoulder and helps us believe in our own beauty and goodness. We set up a war within and outside of ourselves by becoming the one who attacks our own sensitivity and vulnerability. Fear causes us to prey on ourselves. We are the victim hiding from the predator. Yet, we don't realize that we are choosing a *victim mentality*, because it makes someone else the enemy. The enemy is always hiding within us giving us the choice to make it someone else's fault that we are the way we are.

Avoiding that negative conditioning has been one of my major artistic challenges. My paintings, in general, are based on the crossing point between reality and dream, between technique and freedom, and the flow between reflecting and creating. In order to get rid of the habit of over-thinking a painting, and to let the muse do its job. Once forms appear on the canvas, my creativity becomes the freedom within the form, for the positive thrust of the muse allows the fusing of what is unknown with the known. I can create images out of my subconscious without being afraid.

The real challenge is in letting our own awareness awaken to what it needs to do by seeing the childlikeness, the original innocence, the quality that reminds us that it is a little child who leads us. The child within us is taking the adult by the hand encouraging us to have fun and remember what it means to be happy! Spontaneity is remembering the sense of non-attachment that allows our natural impulses to emanate through form, wearing down our fears to break the hold on our creativity in much the same way the waves of the ocean wear away rocks and turn them to sand.

We truly do create our own habitual reality. The ego can be considered as a series of fixed habitual thought patterns, which are a result of a deployment of invisible energy fields that dominate our consciousness. In order to create a balanced life, we need to carefully direct or align our ego with the positive side of the possibilities to free the power and influence of the inner elements which affect and guide our life. These inner elements, which we have discussed in previous chapters, are the heart, the mind and the muse.

The ego needs to merge with the heart as the center of emotions and feelings. When the ego connects with the heart, it becomes part of what develops and expands love and emotion. When we can develop the faith and trust in our own hearts, we will no longer be looking for approval and admiration outside ourselves, and we will no longer develop feelings being better than or less than others. By befriending the positive ego with the heart, we will no longer desperately be seeking love and security from someone or something else, and we will not swing erratically from one mood to another.

When the ego unites with the positive aspects of the mind, it seeks our wellbeing and helps to guide us to pay special attention to our physical existence, to have a regard for our environment and be aware of how it affects us. Positive ego will help us not to play the victim or martyr and not deny that we have a responsibility for what we choose. We can't wait until the world is perfect in order for us to be well and to realize our potential for joy. Uniting the ego with the positive aspects of the mind prevents us from clinging to the past and guides us to face a challenge rather than avoid it by being passive and uncertain. It prevents us from being rigid and inflexible, and it especially helps us to avoid harming and abusing others when we become manipulative and controlling to try to feel powerful.

Connecting the ego with the muse becomes a part of what expands our identity. It prevents us from feeling empty and dissatisfied by enabling the muse to help us to make a change. It is often the negative ego that causes many artists to become addicted to drugs and alcohol as a substitute for the full use of their own imagination. This moves them to rely on something outside of themselves to imitate an artificially stimulated illusion of creativity, just like athletes can rely on artificially developed strength and fitness through the illegal use of steroids. Merging ego with the muse offers a permanent solution to feelings of helplessness by finding a way to appear to be powerful and to take the responsibility to develop one's natural abilities.

When the positive ego merges with the heart, the mind and the muse, it will help us create a meaningful life. The union of the ego with the developing powers of the interior source calls us to be responsible for helping to guide and recognize this. When the ego befriends the mind, the heart experiences the possibility of infinite expansion. The light within the heart connects with the light beyond us. Similar to the way the Sun warms Earth, the rays of light embed something life-giving beneath the soil, when the divine light of love warms our hearts, it unveils the source of love within us.

Ego that is able to connect with the muse in a positive way can uplift humanity by developing creative people like Mozart, Rumi, Da Vinci, Edison, Benjamin Franklin – those who make the kind of contribution that will help us move in a positive direction in our development. This leads to the highly creative and intelligent contribution that can make discoveries that benefit all of mankind.

As human beings, we have been created to allow the ego to work together with our heart, our muse, and our mind. When these are all in unison, they enhance and develop each other, rather than being against one another to cause a war within us. Together, they develop a bridge to our own wholeness. When the perception is basically positive, and there is no internal conflict or selfish motive, we can be guided toward a totally different kind of wisdom in ruling ourselves, and to have integrity to lead others. Without judgment or opinion being the ruling factor, love appears as a kind of inner righteousness that is instinctive, protective, and works toward our wellbeing.

If the ego is at war with the heart, the muse and the mind, it gives power to the negative side of our personality and behavioral tendencies. It can create disaster for humanity through atomic bombs or destructive weapons that could destroy everything and leave little or nothing to be redeemed. It can wipe out an entire city, instead of protecting the lives of its residents.

When ego is acting through negative energy, it is taking a stand and making a declaration to the muse that this is who "I am." This is my identity. I am the one doing the creating. I am the one with a god-like power. That kind of mind can use the illusion of strength to control others. When this happens, the muse gives up and no longer makes an effort to connect us with our creative power. The ego takes over and blocks the creative power from being able to do anything at all. If the thrust of the ego is negatively moved, the muse is unable to help. The mind simply makes a decision by copying another action, or behaving in a way that it has been programmed or conditioned to do, without paying attention to the creative momentum of energy that would urge us to try something new.

If the ego moves the heart with lust and passion, it interferes with creativity by using charm to control through seduction, and we begin to decorate ourselves to gain approval. For example, someone might put on makeup, get a facelift, wear expensive clothes, jewelry, dye their hair, all of which is an attempt to come up with an alluring disguise, instead of being their natural self. Becoming an imitation of something is not part of the creative process, it is a strategy to gain approval and attention. It is ego taking control and trying to overpower the other elements in a negative direction.

When the mind is forced to compete, it doesn't have the creative power to act on its own. It becomes repetitious, which leads to blockage. Many who experience a creative block just react to it by resorting to negative behavior, and they tend to blame others for it. They blame parents, teachers, partners, children, or those who are authority figures that have mistreated them or taught them wrong. They want to personify the evil, objectify it, and make it someone else's fault. Someone else is to blame for their wrongdoing or destructive behavior. This invariably blocks the muse.

Negative ego makes us believe that we are nothing and declares that the ego has all the power. Losing the connection with creativity can be an unbearable burden and it can become difficult to act at all. Often a person becomes depressed and doesn't want to do anything. They have no desire or incentive to create. They become a consumer of goods and services that already exist and believe there is no other alternative at that point. Rainer Maria Rilke wrote, *"Make your ego porous. Will is of little importance, complaining is nothing, fame is nothing. Openness, patience, receptivity, solitude is everything."*

A creative person has vision that could be completely different from anything that has existed before. It is important for everyone to develop an inner strength and courage to creatively express their visions, and to pursue them, regardless of the advice of others to give them up or modify them for their own comfort. If we do not attend to our creative dreams, they will later turn into our self-induced obsessions and ultimately turn against us. If all the great artists who never received recognition in their lifetime, had given up under criticism or social pressure, we would have been deprived of centuries of beauty and insight. Even if we are not great creators, on many different levels our work still contributes something that is just as meaningful when it comes from love.

As our planet is rapidly becoming a global village, we need to find ways to work together to help free every human life, to invite the opening of every human heart, to awaken the mind, and to surrender the ego into the sensitive and positive guidance of the muse. To live a creative life is an incredible grace. We need to do all that we can to find the way to nurture and allow this for every human being, for in doing this we expand the possibilities for all.

The challenge before us is to explore the complexities of the purpose of the ego and how these systems interact and affect each other. If we make the ego the enemy and deny its value in our evolution, we threaten our own survival. When the blocks to our creative power are removed, the way opens for us to consider the positive power of the ego that helps us sustain life and work creatively with the muse, instead of opposing it. This has the potential to help us open new beginnings and to truly become a full partner in developing our own wholeness and creative power.

POWER OF SURRENDER

Don't seek God in temples. He is close to you.
He is within you. Only you should surrender to Him
and you will rise above happiness and unhappiness.

LEO TOLSTOY

CREATIVITY IS AN EXPRESSION OF the playful spirit of the creator. The joy of creating is a source of energy. When the creative act is so filled with power that goes beyond the capability of the individual to handle it, one has to stand by and let it happen or surrender to it and allow the power to sweep them away as it expresses itself.

The word 'surrender' generally means to yield to a controlling power. In English, it has been mainly associated with ceasing resistance to an enemy or opponent and submitting to their authority, especially as a prisoner, or a defeated soldier, or even to a feeling of despair. This interpretation of surrender is not associated with positive action. When we hear, "surrender in the name of the law," it usually means trouble. Even in a battle or an argument, when one side surrenders to another, it is a sign that they have given up any hope for victory.

Just like the word 'ego,' surrender has positive and negative meanings. The positive meaning is to willingly submit to a superior or divine power, rather than a competitive opponent, in the knowledge that power will watch out for us in a much more effective and positive way than we can do ourselves. It is when a believer willingly gives up their own will and subjects their thoughts, ideas and deeds to the will and guidance of a higher power.

In most religions, surrender and obedience are primary values of faith, superseded only by an unconditional love for God and all creation. One of the meanings of the word 'Islam' is surrender, which is submitting all responsibilities of one's life to Allah and living in accordance to the will of God. Every single action in a Muslim's life, whether it is marriage, buying a house or building a career is theoretically for the sake of Allah. This is a theological belief that manifests as a faith and guide for believers.

In psychology, the word surrender is often used as an antonym of hostility, suggesting something similar to accepting one's own nature as being of the world. In the creative process, surrender is willful acceptance and yielding to the governing power of the muse. Reflecting or somehow manifesting that power in a new way generates the excitement that the creator feels.

Surrendering to higher consciousness is to synchronize with the creative power, which is energized by the grace of the heart and the muse. Some creative people are naturally attracted to the thrill of the manifestation of the creative act. Others are drawn to surrender to the direction of the muse. Whatever we do, we need to enter into the process with our whole hearts. When we do, we taste the sweetness of love. It is in surrendering that we commune with our own deeper nature. It reveals the kind of truth that can become a faith, a cultural belief, or a way of life.

So many voices flow through us, so many faces reveal themselves to us and so many feelings enter our hearts, that we have no capability of sustaining all the wonder and complexity of them. We are a part of a greatness that rises and expands beyond what our physical expressions can contain. If we call this expansion God or the Creator, we personify it. When we call it the muse, we are giving the same greatness to the force and existence of the creative power, but we open the name and identity to be discerned by the heart, rather than by a theological belief. The difference is that, in the creative process, we activate our own relationship with it through surrendering, and we say yes in a consensual way that affirms our belonging.

When something attracts me, whether it is a part of nature or some artistic work, I often go and paint to let the beauty that has touched me flow freely and even wildly from the well of desire that is guided by my muse. In doing so, I focus on developing images that I can intuit or perceive, and at the same time, I surrender to a stream of power that reveals forms and shapes that are beyond what I can discover on my own. One fuels the other, and I have to have faith in that power and trust the muse to guide me in both dimensions, or, at least, sustain my awareness of it. It is a willful act of yielding to something unseen, an act of surrendering to a streaming energy that sweeps me into the creative flow. If I close off the potentials out of fear of the unknown, the creative flow stops.

Those who strive for tight control over their lives, have a fear of facing what is unknown to them. Surrendering allows the guidance that reveals itself gently and compassionately as a friend. When we try to claim the power for ourselves without surrendering, we are totally out of our element and out of alignment with the highest power that sustains the universe. We can cooperate with the source and become partners with it to create likenesses, produce new life, and build giant dams. We can harness the sun in generators, but we can't become the single source that created the original fire that sparked a universe. There is far too much that is unknown to us to make claim to being the 'Creator of All things.' We may feel God-like when we love and nurture the life of others, but this is an empowering stream moving freely through our surrendered hearts.

As the creative power flows through us, we are continually being transformed and experiencing new birth. We sleep with it, we walk with it in the gardens and meadows of life and we lie down under the stars with it to discover its power moving through us. Thus, we are transported by it and bring the newness of our hearts to it. The wildness that is released within us sometimes is so original that we might think we are meeting a new being or a new energy. Yet, it expresses more of the reality of our own hearts than anything we can imagine.

When we surrender to the flow of creativity, we actively and creatively seek to find expression for the inexpressible, allowing the exotic blossoms along the path to flourish. During this period, in most cases, we are not even a person with an identity in any way we can recognize. We become aligned with the creative power, and the experience is so enlarged, so expanded, it has nothing to do with the tiny ego self, operating in the darkness of our fear of the unknown.

Artists are those who reach for union with life through their connection with creation. The surrendering process of creating draws them into the fullness and receptivity of the heart and to the guidance of the muse. It also draws the artist into the positive aspects of the mind in a way that all is surrendered to the life-giving light and energy of the source of all creation, in the body and the soul. Nothing can remain separate from it. Images that show up on canvas or in the sound of music, mirrors what the artist feels. The canvas or the instruments of expression disappear, and the angels appear. They are here and everywhere, and the light fills the heart of the artist who is in love with the beloved that he is creating.

Those who are fully surrendered to their inner power of the muse, do what they do out of submission without the full understanding of the mystery, because they cannot handle the fullness of the truth as they live it. So, in the process, they create their own myth. Even the great ones throughout history had to surrender in faith, and act without full understanding. If they had known about the mystery and what was about to happen, they would not be able to respond in the same way. Think of Alexander the Great, or Moses, or Jesus, and how they had to act on faith to do much of what they did. If they had known ahead of time exactly what was going to happen, they probably would not have been able to move ahead. Through surrender they received assurance to follow the inner wisdom that was flowing through them.

Many people tell us they are surrendered, but they also tell us how they chose a safe way to journey through the challenges they have faced. Jesus didn't know the fullness of the truth while it was happening. He may have sensed it, intuited it, and surrendered to the muse of a 'creator father' with which he found his relatedness and a sense of belonging. We look at it in hindsight, and like the physicists, we search for theories to explain it. Jesus was true to his experience, and he created his own mythology and his own stories, as we all do. Yet, sometimes we stretch and manipulate it to be what we want it to be, so we can understand, control and use it to our own purpose. Learning from the parables may mean being open to a creative response that we may not be able to fully understand or express.

I often look at what I have painted and realize I didn't create it alone. It came through me, and I am fascinated by the power that it reveals. I am excited by it. My temperature rises, and I feel the flames from the fire of creativity. The spirit within me guides me through the feelings that flow through my heart to create a vision to express it.

Surrendering is to have total faith in the process that everything is possible. It is to have faith that a bird without wings could develop wings and experience flight, or that a fish in the sea can move onto the land and become a land animal. Darwin saw this physically happening when the creatures took the first steps from the water to the land. They adapted to the change and lived into a new way of being. They followed their hunger to a new land, as we surrender to our own hunger and longing to lead us to a new realm. We share the inspiration with Moses as he tells his story of being guided to a new land by a source he could not see, yet he could feel through the creative power of his faith. As he surrendered to it, he was able to lead the Israelites out of oppression and captivity.

Artists, prophets and explorers all gain expertise and authority from their total surrendering. They have vision that empowers the positive muse to guide them and open the door to the dream of life that exists just beyond reality. They create metaphors and myths to move them. We learn to act beyond what we know through surrendering, as we follow the muse into the unknown. There is no goal that we cannot reach, precisely because there is no set goal that even exists. It is a symbol of what is not yet created. It will change a hundred times before we reach it. When we are surrendered, we keep moving, keep going, and we find ourselves in the flow. We set in motion that great spirit of wisdom within us, and we become aware that we are all part of a greater creative power. Without realizing it, we may react out of ignorance, and we contaminate the purity of our own innocence, which is quite a different quality.

We carry the concept of the impossible into our vocabularies, and we cry out that we are too young, too weak, too old, too limited, not realizing that the *intelleto* or the divine power is already flowing through us. We exist within the divine power, and we enter into the experience of what Paul Gauguin meant when he said, *"I create; therefore I am God."* Yet the artist is often misunderstood with his creative, mythological and iconic language and symbols for divine power.

Creating art is not about developing a business. It is about going inside the self and expanding to connect with the muse and hopefully, through the heart uniting with other hearts. It is about being creative in life, and allowing the perspective to be expanded until it shoots out in all directions like the sun to create something new. As German Expressionist artist Franz Mark said, *"Art is nothing but the expression of our dream; the more we surrender to it the closer we get to the inner truth of things, our dream-life, the true life that scorns pointless questions and does not even see them."*

Every human being is designed to carry certain divine messages within them. These are concepts that we create through our subconscious, and this is the way we express what we feel most deeply. We explore, and we try to unveil the clues to reveal the images within us. Everyone has a unique way to do that. For Michelangelo, it was chipping away the extra marble to release *David*. We seek to rise out of the stone under the caressing hands of love. We ache to be born out of the music sounding out from within us. We coax the truth from the canvas of our own souls.

Creativity flows from the mystery of soul into physical expression, from the unknown to the known, from darkness to light, all the while the concepts co-exist within us. It is a spectrum that flows from intensity to stillness and from expansion to contraction. To create something is to surrender to the fullness of the whole range of our deeper feelings. We *leila* and play with ideas until something begins to manifest. This is true in art as well as in life. If it attracts us, we eliminate whatever does not feel like it belongs. The muse removes and enhances the developing concept. Hopefully, ideas are guided by the heart and the mind, which together know the way of truth within each one of us.

Next time you encounter a unique creation, notice what is attracting and producing a feeling of response in you. When you are creating, be attentive to what appeals to you as it emerges. Pay attention to what entices you to surrender to its flow. Let it evolve within you, allow a shift to take place, and you will suddenly begin expressing something new. You soften toward it. Your mood changes and you are drawn into what it is revealing. Your editing muse enhances it and develops it so you are able to share the experience with others.

As you continue the process, you learn to release what you think you know, and discover what is inside you seeking to be expressed. You will begin to 'unlearn' what you have so carefully itemized and catalogued in your mind as knowledge, and you will remove what does not seem to belong. This is the way to eliminate what is keeping us out of balance and what spoils the harmony and meaning of the deeper messages hiding within us.

A yearning to allow creativity to flow through us is embedded within everyone. A guide or a coach can only help to draw this out. The way is not determined by what someone else tells us we should do. We follow our inner muse to guide us in the way that moves us toward the greatest teacher of all other teachers, which is the creative power of love. In truth, love is the only teacher. A few moments of doing whatever we are doing with love is worth an entire year of acquiring knowledge with the self-professed experts

Inspiration that fires imagination lasts for only a moment. It is the light that ignites the fire that gives birth to a creative form. If a person simply hangs on to the inspiration, he has already fallen out of the flow. Creativity happens through surrendering to the movement. If we are not expressing in complete freedom, we are not truly creating, we are simply constructing or making something practical or useful. It is the journey that creates the life, the electrifying flash of connection that turns an illusion into something real. The moment the feelings take over, is the moment we are free to create. We can then zero in on the variety of ways possible to manifest those feelings in a unique form.

When I begin a new painting, I stand before the canvas and look for what might be hidden in the depths of the blank canvas. I gaze into it, to envision and to feel what is hidden in the mystery. I am curious to find out what is there, seeking to be expressed.

This is quite different than beginning to paint with a certain thing already in mind. As I *leila* and play with paint, my subconscious draws something into my vision that wants to reveal itself. There is a moment, a wonderful moment, when I cannot identify myself as separate from this process. At that point, I feel as if I were floating in a creative current, allowing it to take me wherever it wants to go. The colors begin to intensify, and the canvas becomes all energy, rather than a flat surface. I have fallen into the ecstasy of love. I have only one response, and that is to surrender. If I fail to do this, I will miss the joy for which I was created.

When I am fully surrendered, I become totally bewildered and lose my bearings. I do not feel a mental connectedness to the unknown in any rational way. Love whispers in my ear to come toward it, fall into it, and let everything shift to expand and express the moment. It is where the sweetness is found. It is the most thrilling occurrence that I experience in my life. Every time I go through the process, I am given new clues by which I will recognize it more quickly the next moment love calls.

Surrendering to the creative flow is to bring whatever we are feeling into some form of expression and let it manifest what it wants to reveal. Mystics call such a feeling the whispering of the heart. We learn to listen to it, while keeping the mind free from evaluating anything. Rather than changing things, we let love make the shift. The flow doesn't let us to stop and analyze. The wind loves the tree as it blows through the leaves, mingling in its branches. The river loves the rocks to experience the flow around them. This is the power that allows us to *leila*, to dance in the playground of love. Love transforms everything and becomes the music of the lover's song.

How long the process lasts, and how far it goes, is completely irrelevant. When the creative act becomes too overpowering, we simply surrender to it and enjoy experiencing what is manifesting through whatever medium we are using. As we experience the joy, the creation becomes filled with grace, because our soul is continually anointing and energizing it with love.

When we allow surrender, we communicate with the surrendered. It may become a school, a faith, a religion, or a cultural belief system. Here is where creative peaks turn creators into mindless lovers. It is impossible to distinguish whether it is the spiritual energy that is moving through, or it is the physical energy that is reflecting it. One without the other leaves no way to differentiate between the two, which is the wonderful reality of why we are drawn to love each other.

When we surrender to the creative flow, the joy that emanates and surrounds us helps to develop the spirit, to become ageless, and to expand us as lovers. Just like the rose that blooms to reveal the uniqueness of its seed, creative power spreads an aroma and beauty far beyond our perception of its gift.

What continuously attracts us to surrender is our longing. Every time we experience longing, we encourage the flow and we fall into its streaming creative energy. When joy appears in the act of lovemaking, it rises and falls in waves of feeling like the deep rhythms of the sea reaching for shore. Our joy seeks complete balance, beyond volume or size. The issue is not that bigger is better as it has to do with how two energies correspond with each other, and how they commune and unite into one. How it all happens is one of the deep secrets cradled in the mysteries of creation.

I am often asked if I will teach someone how to make certain practical images on the canvas. My response is almost always the same. Being an artist is not about learning how to make images, it is about surrendering to the creative flow. We think of technique as making our creativity perfect, but there is no perfection where comparison exists. Creativity becomes a problem when we imitate and copy in order to be accepted, because perfection has very little to do with creativity.

The development of my creative energy has not been oriented toward reaching a certain goal, nor has it been about perfecting a certain practice. In fact, it does not lean toward any goal. I have not made a mission statement, and I don't have a business card, for my creative life is not a business. I flow with the energy and let it guide me. I surrender to what I do, because I love it. The energy I receive is my reward. I *leila*, I play, and the energies are limitless and exhilarating. I feel and tune into a spiritual energy that coordinates with a physical energy. There is always playfulness, and the joy comes when I make a connection with the deep roots of my beginnings. Our roots help to make us unique and allow a glimpse of the process of individuation. Without that, we would lose the beauty of variety. Oneness contains the wonder of variation without separating us.

Someone recently asked me if I was a professional artist, and I had to think about it. I am sure the answer I gave them is not the answer they expected. Professionalism develops a rigid form, and it creates a barrier or a shield around a person. As a professional, you deal with certain standards set up or established by others, or they may be standards that you set up for yourself. The moment we set professionalism as our goal, we begin to lose the playful spirit that comes with the freedom of surrendering. When we fail to do that, we put a wall around the playground, fence it in, and we place limits on our creative energy.

We deal with something that is called competence. Joy helps us do what we intend to do. For example, let's say we are talking about creating something unique in a certain field of design. We can be creative, but it includes limitations of the body, the involvement of interior and exterior, and the limits of walls and spaces. Architecture deals with limitations of land and safety codes. Aerodynamics considers the lengths of strength and wingspan.

How do we surrender to the creative act to manifest? If we only let the creative act lead us into manifesting, we lose much of our creativity and our joy, because we are forced to focus our energy on the limitations. If we freely create without limitation from the beginning, once we have created the overall concept, we can manifest it into the limitation of form without compromising our creative ability.

We reach for a constant flow whether it is in poetry, in music, or in setting a dinner table. When I am painting, each one of the images that appears on my canvas is an expression of some aspect of the soul. It is moved by my surrendering to the muse. Sometimes, I feel that I don't have the ability to paint a certain image, and when that happens, I usually end up painting with doubt and lose the feeling of joy in what I am doing.

When we surrender to the muse and are in the flow, the creative act and the manifestation happen simultaneously. It is a kind of transformation. We learn to change the rhythm in the dance of creating, improvising in every moment. Many of those who have written or talked about the creative process will sometimes offer guidelines to follow in order to be creative. That is developing a technique that has been formed to follow, which teaches control instead of creativity. To create, we need to be inspired and learn to surrender to our muse.

It is true that creativity needs a structure, some kind of development or system, for we need to find a way to manage the results. Yet structure by itself is not creative. We can move without rhythm and expression, but if we put the rhythm and expression to the movement, it becomes a dance. It reveals a most important difference.

We develop a faith that guides us to surrender freely to the creative flow. There are infinite possibilities in a drop of sperm, and those that are not used are expendable. We can always learn something about surrendering from nature, for it doesn't concern itself by considering any form as indispensable to the process of creation. The potential to manifest simply continues to flow and create, for that is its nature. When we can learn to embrace living with joy in this same way, we invite the energy of creativity into our entire existence! Our surrender into the creative process deeply affects the quality and wonder of how we live and how we love.

POWER OF SILENCE

Only when you drink from the river of silence shall you indeed sing.
And when you have reached the mountain top, then you shall begin to climb.
And when the earth shall claim your limbs, then shall you truly dance.

KHALIL GIBRAN

SILENCE IS THE DWELLING PLACE of creation, thus creative process begins and ends in silence. It holds the mystery and surprise of all that is created. Every word evolves from silence, every sound proceeds from silence, and everything that is created has originated from silence. The essence of love and creativity exists in silence and not in the words that are derived from the rational mind.

Scripture tells us, *"In the beginning was the Word, and the Word was with God, and the Word was God."* This is a powerful metaphor alluding to the great silence rather than spoken words. In the beginning, there was no one to speak. It was a process unfolding in silence or a divine decree that manifested in a creative result. This is an indication that the divine power, or the power of creativity, is a profound intention arising from silence.

The greatest of human creations have not evolved from the words expressed by a person manifesting greatness, but from the depth of the silence of pure intention. In fact, the infinite universe is expressed through silence. God is the name given to the unlimited eternal energy that is always creating and that which is beyond boundaries, time, place, words, and all comprehension. While God is not known through the mind, we discover a deep well and a fountain inside us through which God may be experienced as a divine touch igniting us with divine love.

Silence is the ultimate presence of the creative flow to all that exists, and all that has not yet appeared in existence. As living creatures, we keep a vigil of love in reverent silence in response to the overwhelming gift of love that has offered us life. Unable to hold it inside, we break out in praise and celebration of the beauty of that love. Words can sometimes dissipate power rather than strengthen it. In many cases, the loss of power is the result of talking about the intention before it has resulted in manifestation.

Silence is not merely the absence of sound. Silence can be a deafeningly loud call to create and achieve without the frantic hurry to get past one achievement to another. Silence can open a space to listen, to listen to the silence, to hear the gap in the void created by the lack of noise. Silence allows for communication not with others but with the self and all the ideas that grow out of discovering an authentic personality.

Life is illuminated when lips are closed and the heart speaks. Silence enhances power. It is the pride of the humble and the humility of the proud. It is the zenith of merit for the brave and the haven of security for the coward. Silence is the wisdom of fools and the discretion of the wise. It is the basis for the development of character. It is the mystery and the voice within the heart that leads to reverence, patience, self-control, endurance, and courage.

No one can create without silence and stillness, without the inner solitude that demands a deep and intentional listening to feelings. Among all the mystic poets, Rumi has given more focus and value to 'silence' for those on the path of enlightenment than any other. Much of his poetry ends with the words, *"Be silent"* or some other descriptive phrase about being silent. His most mystical poems and those with deeper meanings often reflect the importance of silence. Perhaps some of the best advice in his poetry is when he tells himself to be silent as he feels the emergence of the rational mind interfering with his ecstatic state. He usually stops the poetry and goes into silence when that happens. He describes the condition thus:

I am devoted to Love.

Speak to me of nothing but love.

Only talk of sweetness and light

or say nothing.

To Rumi, nothing is worth saying if what is said is not spoken out of love that flows freely through the heart to guide what is being said. In fact, poetry to him is conversation with love. It is in silence that love most easily finds the way to the heart. It is in silence that love is given the freest passage. The expression of the message then has the perfect clarity of truth. If we open our mouths to speak, and our words do not come from love, then we should say nothing.

Silence has many concealed advantages in the creative process. The simplest one is that it relieves apprehension and doubt, and frees a person to embrace an inner peace that leads to creativity. Silence is pure essence, while talking is like a cover surrounding the essence. The deep ecstasy of the spiritual journey harbors the beauty that is hidden inside.

Every human being has the creative power to send out thoughts that inspire, heal and warm the heart. The sublime overtone that is heard in a concerto or images that are hidden in the brushstroke of a painter are secret points of entry that lead to the light which is hidden within us and grows more luminous in the time of silence. Without the prelude of deep silence, there is hardly anything to say that matters.

Sometimes, creativity is not a manifested expression, but a silence that can either break us down or become a relief to heal us. Eventually, the difference between suffering and healing is the difference between torturing ourselves for not being able to create and sitting still in an uncomfortable silence. So, what happens when we stop creating and become silent?

When I'm not creating, I feel a period of non-doing is happening in my life. As the days of not creating begin to increase, it becomes vital for me to listen intently to my muse and my heart, and forget for a while all the logical excuses that rule my mind and provoke doubts about my creative abilities. As I let that happen, a transformation, usually a serious one, occurs in my life. This transformation is always creative, whether I recognize it or not. Something creative happens, even when I don't create, which is in the silence, for it feels the missing energy. Inside me, energy is seeking a path where it can thrive and begin to manifest an emerging form that is seeking expression. My task is to clear away the superfluous distractions, and let the energy pour forth like a river rushing through. Franz Kafka wrote, *"You do not need to do anything; you do not need to leave your room. Remain sitting at your table and listen. You do not even need to listen; just wait. You do not even need to wait; just become still, quiet and solitary and the world will freely offer itself to you to be unmasked. It has no choice. It will roll in ecstasy at your feet."*

When we are sitting in stillness and listening intently to the silence in our lives, stripped of ego, and befriending the muse, it doesn't mean we have stopped creating. It simply means we are giving space to the creative power to emerge. It is like the hibernating instinct of animals. Creativity is an energy that does not diminish. We simply place a dam in front of its flow to store the energy for the future. The next thing to do is to redirect the creative flow and make a channel to guide it to pour out and reveal itself in some unique way. The expression comes through when we invoke a faith, which invites the truth to reveal itself through silence and creative transformation.

The first and most appropriate action is to completely stop thinking about how or when or where the desired result will manifest, and simply trust that the silent power of intention sets into motion the best possible process to achieve the desired result. At that point, one has to just let go, return to the silence of selflessness, and listen for guidance and surrender to what comes through. There is energy in silence that can make us think and feel, make us act, slow down the influence of the mind, and help us to surrender to the creative process.

As a creative person, I welcome silence or what the Italians call, *dolce far niente*, sweet doing nothing. It eliminates my distractions, and compels me to be alone with myself. Silence has the gift of helping us discover the most profound and meaningful inner pleasures. When we bask in the joy of silence, we learn how to relish and value life by effectively incorporating solitude in it.

Usually, we become so accustomed to the noise and sounds around us that until our attention is drawn to the grace of silence, we are not aware of how noise has invaded our space. Aside from that, we become so used to the absence of silence, that many people feel uncomfortable when they have to face it. They think silence is a void and they have to fill it with chatter, with the sound of radio, television and music, or noise of some kind. Silence can make people feel uncomfortable and alone. My aunt has to have her television on, even though most of the time she does not watch it, especially when she is in a deep sleep. She feels secure when she has the background noise of television. For many people, it is a buffer against the chattering voice mulling over the concerns of the mind.

The pure pleasure of listening to the inner voice takes place during silent times. When we maintain silence for a day or a major part of the day, we experience the phenomenon of solitude. That is when we can truly appreciate the input we receive from our surroundings as we draw energy from being silent. Some of the best times to create are during those silent times.

My most creative time starts from ten o'clock at night, when no one bothers me, even on the phone, until about two to three in the morning. At those times, I immerse in my muse and I have little awareness of anything happening around me. I usually listen to music, sometimes the same melody repeats for hours without my noticing it. My silence could easily be interrupted if I listen to a song with words. I listen to instrumental music without words or, if there are lyrics, they are in languages that I am not able to understand or process with my mind. This is how I develop a tranquil environment where silence overpowers lots of busy and noisy information that I would otherwise carry in my mind.

Another way that silence helps to enhance creativity is how it allows us to observe details. When our mind is busy either talking or listening, we miss seeing much of what is around us. Perhaps this is one reason why many artists paint from nature by going to it, or why the portrait artists remain silent while they are painting. When we are busy in a conversation, many fine details that are available for our eyes to see, are eliminated because the mind's capacity for attentiveness is not available to see them. Keeping the mind clear of clutter and giving it the silence and space to observe all there is to see is extremely vital to bring out all those crucial details.

Silence is the source that gives voice to our soul. When we are talking or preparing to talk, we can no longer hear the song within. A calmer mind is reflected during silence. Imagination flourishes as it provides a chance to grow from feelings within. Creativity of any sort, such as painting, poetry, music and science are homage we pay to silence.

Inspiration of any kind comes when there is peace of mind. Often times, people feel they need to search outside for inspiration, while in fact, it is right inside of them. All they need to do is to seek out a quiet place and listen until eventually they are surprised by what they hear. Sometimes I wonder what would have happened to science if the apple that hit Isaac Newton in the head had fallen from the rooftop of a house in a crowded city, rather than while he was sitting in a quiet place under a tree. He most likely would have tried to find who threw it, instead of reflecting on what made it fall.

Living in the midst of too much noise is bound to have some negative effect on creativity. Most noises that are heard in today's social environment are fundamentally disturbing. The sound of birds singing or of the wind rushing through the apple trees is pleasant, and it may have empowered Newton's muse to create, but mechanical noises are mostly disturbing. Those who live in a crowded environment and against a background of mechanical noise, usually develop a subliminal feeling of agitation inside them, which can become a source of so much anxiety! This is probably one of the reasons why modern music and art have lost the tranquility they used to offer in the past.

Today, our senses are filled with external stimuli. Our visions are crowded with constantly shifting scenes, and our ears are attacked by a variety of sounds, all of which have great impact on our mind, muse and heart. We become drained of energy and lose the tranquility that is needed for us to create. We need to give more time to relaxing and letting our energy become renewed through natural means.

The same way that the natural calmness and tranquility of the outside world has been covered over by mechanical noise, sometimes peace of mind becomes disturbed by the chattering of a negative ego. This chattering includes an endless flow of worries, fears, doubtful thoughts, negative dreams, memories, inner debate and all that occupies the mind from morning to evening. This noise from within is what gets people into trouble when they give too much attention to small inconveniences or uncertainties and make them important factors in their life. This constant inner chattering prevents them from living in the moment and giving their full attention to their surroundings and to the activities of their lives. When negativities that block relatedness are eliminated, deeper connections take place in positive ways.

SILENCING THE MUSE

Everyone is endowed with creative ability that can be exercised in either the physical realm or in the spiritual realm. The manifestation of it requires solid intention, appropriate action and the capability to implement it. The way to prevent clutter in the mind is to make sure all three of these abilities are utilized.

There are times when these three activities are not all in full operation. Sometimes we are lacking the ability to complete our creation, other times we are too weary to continue, and further action is needed to finish it. If this happens, the muse becomes exhausted by trying to do something. The emotions of an individual move them toward inactivity, toward being passive and unresponsive. The person may become lazy and not do anything except to become a consumer.

Under these circumstances, not doing something can be more productive than to keep on trying when nothing is happening. There are times that I keep on repeating painting something just to wash it off when it isn't working. If I am not satisfied, I keep doing that until I lose my energy. When I face this reality, my movement becomes limited and I begin to regress and interrupt the flow of what was happening. I become filled with regret, exhausted and I finally give up. I let go of the painting and leave my studio to do something else to let my mind shift away from what I was doing. Scientists call this entropy – life collapsing in on itself.

If I quit trying and just relax without searching for a solution before entropy sets in, I can rest my case. When I rest, I am able to allow my energy to renew itself. I build toward the challenge to take a new leap, to be free enough to try something new. Ansel Adams said, *"When words become unclear, I shall focus with photographs. When images become inadequate, I shall be content with silence."*

In most cases, being away from what we were creating becomes more productive than experimenting and trying to do something when we are not quite ready to express it. While we are resting, we may think it is wasting time, but all the while, it is giving us a chance to see what we couldn't see before. Breaking away from what we have been unsuccessfully trying to do, and coming back to it at some later time allows us to take a new look and see things differently. It is a little like going to a new depth, a place of no return, because it changes us. We are done with 'outsight' and we begin 'insight' which is looking within to begin a new journey that could lead us toward recovery.

When a new insight is developed, the creative movement begins to accelerate and suddenly a new choice is born. As soon as I experience that, I go back to my studio and what I was trying to achieve in my painting takes on a whole new look. One brushstroke on the canvas completes the painting and develops the image. All the time that I was frustrated, repeatedly trying something and washing it off, I was waiting for that one stroke. The painting wasn't finished, because I had worn myself out, looking for a solution that needed more energy than I had to bring to it. I needed more creative power to see the wholeness of the image.

When I return to what I was painting, I am filled with new insight. I am relaxed, and my subconscious takes over. My inner reality sees it differently, and I can get my outer reality, my outer perspective of the experience, out of the way. The painting has not changed but I have, after relaxing and allowing the insight to come through. A period away from something is rarely wasted. It is absolutely necessary, because it offers a new energy that revitalizes and connects us to the creative flow.

The most creative moments of life come when there is a new vision, a startling new perception, and an awakening surprise, which evolve after moving away from pressure.

It is the best possible time to allow something new to be born. It is the best time to make babies, the best time to cook something new, the best time to paint, or write, or make music. We learn to recognize the moment, and we make the jump. We break the rules, and we pave the way for something new and exciting to happen. If we don't move forward to meet it, we live with regret.

In a game of basketball, when the players are all running toward the basket, there is an intense push toward the basket, and suddenly one player leaps in the air, turns and reaches the goal in a movement of grace. He causes a shift in the action, relieves the pressure he is feeling by finding a new freedom, and he does it through a sudden leap into the air. In that moment, he has a clear vision of the basket. The player has had no time to plan that, it is an instinctive response. He takes a risk. He leaps free of the push of the crowd running at full speed in the competition to be there first, and he jumps, stands alone above the rest, and in an arc of freedom, he takes on a new action.

Most creative people, discoverers and inventors tell us how something new came to them after they were at the end of their rope, trying over and over to solve something in the conventional ways. They took a valuable leap, after they moved away and relaxed into the new vision or the new invention.

Relaxing is different from laziness. Just lazing around can be completely unproductive. The more time a person spends thinking about the problem, the bigger the problem becomes. In many countries across the globe, businesses take a siesta after lunch to break away from what they were doing. After they return from the siesta, they usually shift their program into something new.

During the siesta for the Sufi, reflection becomes a spiritual development. If an apprentice is working with a master or a mentor, it is absolutely necessary to have some time away to come back and receive the final lesson. This is often the guidance that allows the apprentice to visualize the highest perspective, to experience the wholeness. After he comes into the fullness of his own truth, he leaves the master to integrate the truth he has learned into his own life.

There are special holidays, feasts, and holy days in most religions. The majority of people think those days are for remembrance. The holiday is less about remembering than about taking a break away from repetition. We relax, watch the sunrise, and we allow ourselves time to relax. It prepares us to make a shift and to build up the energy needed to do it. When we are relaxed, we are not resisting. We are not fighting against what needs to happen. That is when creativity is possible.

Some people paint to relax before creating music. Some play music to relax before painting. We each need to find what helps to relax us, to relieve the tensions we build up. Surrendering is to move into that warmer place where it is possible to relax, and the ultimate place of surrender is in the arms of love. There is a sacred silence in the soul, which in its ultimate freedom is the beloved. Love introduces us to the beloved within us, and we are home! Whatever we call it, it is being at home in the soul. It is there we can truly develop our creative power!

POWER OF CREATIVITY

To cease to think creatively is only slightly different from ceasing to live.

BENJAMIN FRANKLIN

CREATION IS THE MANIFESTATION OF the playful spirit of a creator having fun. True joy is achieved when a person is in such a state of creative flow. It is like being on a playground where one wishes to stay forever. Unfortunately, no matter how long we play, there comes a time when we are called to leave the playground. As soon as we do, a reversal of energy takes place that diminishes the joy. The creative play that was deeply energizing begins to weaken and fade, and often leads to feelings of weariness, exhaustion, and sometimes depression. It is difficult to maintain the enthusiasm for a long time, because the creative process continues only as long as it is manifesting some kind of beauty and balance in its movement – similar to the rising and falling waves of love.

Sometimes the creative play is filled with such power that it goes beyond one's capacity to handle it. This is when there is a need for complete surrender to an inner guidance to allow the momentum of the stream of creative energy to express itself. When we are able to reflect the energy, to be a passage for it, we allow it to manifest in new ways, and we are privileged to experience the excitement and variation of creation itself. We synchronize with the flow of creation energy, and we are inspired and energized by the grace and beauty of experiencing our own soul.

There are times when we are attracted to the thrill of manifesting, and times when we are drawn to surrender into the natural movement in the direction of its flow. Whatever course we take, we need to enter into the process with an open heart to experience the ecstasy and to breathe in the sweetness of love.

Everyone is creative in some unique way, but artists catch the fire and find a path of creative energy that leads them to becoming constant lovers. They enjoy combining the creative play with its expression when they come together in harmony with the natural flow of the universe. We are each different in how we are attracted to the creative process, and for some, it can seem overwhelming. It can be difficult to distinguish whether it is a spiritual energy that is moving through us, or if it is physical energy and sensual being that is reflecting it.

Living a creative life means bringing together the time that we are creating with the times when we are renewing and away from this exhilarating flow. We need to be sensitive and discerning to seek a harmony in the rhythm of how we live in such changing conditions. The creative life begins as both working in harmony with each other and with us subconsciously allowing a transformation to occur. We surrender into a flow that allows the alchemy of both creating and renewing to find a fullness of life.

The creative challenge is to unite the two opposite energies by fusing the differences into a colorful expression of the marvelous variation of life itself. Hopefully, we are able to utilize the unique and distinct qualities of our own natures at the same time that we feel at one with all life. If we feel unable to do this, if we fail to surrender into the natural rhythms of the elements of creation, we miss one of the most thrilling opportunities of this life, which is to be a part of the rich flow of creation itself. We may try to substitute our own versions of living in a way that makes us feel secure and safe by avoiding the changes that can upset us, but it falls short of what is possible when we risk living truly creative lives.

Love is the only creative power that can unite the periods of exalting creativity with the human need for renewal and surrender. It is this awareness that helps us make the leap into the fullness and truth of living creatively. Love is what attracts us, lures and entices us to dwell side by side with all that exists, whether it is like us or not. Life continually invites us to become aware of what is possible if we are open to change. There is always a potential that is unknown and untapped within us. If we hold back because we are afraid, we miss the wonder of discovery.

Mastering creative power requires that we allow creativity to flow continuously through us, and that we are free to manifest what we create in new ways. Energy and the process of expressing it, work together when we love what we are doing and surrender to our muse. We fall into a glorious expression of color, form and beauty that offers us infinite possibilities and the gift of creating something unique. One truly enhances the depth and the experience of the other. If we try to separate these, we weaken the variety and beauty of both.

We are both human and divine, and we move through a kaleidoscope of emotions and feelings when we risk the adventure of mastering our creativity. The more open we can be to the amazing journey of creation, the more we are catapulted into the sublime wonder of everyday life. Love longs to turn us loose in the marvelous wilderness of the unknown to experience loving. To create is to be free to join the creator in the celebration of the ever-expanding vision to make a new world out of our dreams and longings.

Making our own garden of paradise in a corner of the world where we live can fill us with a wonderful sense of wellbeing in everyday life. A mother baking a cake decorated with all the things her child loves expands her own heart when she does this with love. Building a home for someone who is homeless can challenge and expand our vision as well as allow us to do something kind for another human being. There is no limit to the ways we can merge with the impulse to create, if we allow love to guide us.

When a child kicks down a castle of sand on the beach, stomps it into the ground and destroys it, he is making room for the vision of building a new one. The fun is in creating the castle, not in turning it into a stone monument for us to spend the rest of our lives trying to protect.

Love knows our creative nature, is mindful of our potential and what we have to offer, where we have been, how we were formed, and is aware that it decorates the world with the best of who we are. Let love take your hand and lead you where you could never go alone! The beloved is beckoning to you from every side, luring you into your own beautiful self. Love is trying to bring about your transformation to help you do this. It will prune you, cleanse you, burn away what is imprisoning you. Allow the chisel and the hammer to chip away the negative protections you carry around that keep you from seeing the beauty around you and especially the beauty within you.

The act of creation is discovered in the rhythmic flow of creativity. When we become lovers, we no longer separate the act of making love from the energy and flow of love itself. Surrender to love and let making love to life become the way you live.

Whatever we create, we need to fill it with love in all its forms, for when we do that, every single person becomes a true artist of the sacrament of expression of the life force. We partake of it as the manna from Heaven, the bread of life that fell from Heaven as Moses led his people across the desert.

Every living creature on earth is an artist in some sense, and those who create out of that vision discover their own wholeness and form a partnership with the divine creator. Uniting with the divine creator is to live a mission of protecting all of life by loving it. Anyone who feels the sweetness of being loved, seen and known on a deeper level, even for a moment, has glimpsed the beauty and experienced the embrace of the beloved. Such a feeling of love brings total surrender.

The life of creativity beckons us to face three primary challenges: to love, to surrender to love, and to allow ourselves to be loved. There is a mutuality that flows freely and naturally to others and returns to us, when we have discovered a clear path to our own heart. The secret of creative living is found hidden in the dust on the path to wherever we are going. If we add the lubricant of love, we see that the teeming microbes in that rich, wet, and fertile soil are moving and stirring, just waiting for the right moment to spring into life. We are the stuff of that soil, and if we add love to the substance that we are, we will spring into life, take gulps of fresh air, drink deeply of the beauty of life, shout out and sing a song of resounding joy to the world.

Bravery doesn't only happen on the battlefields of war. It happens when our dual natures have to face off and allow our differences to exist within us and find some kind of peace without separation. We can't continue to project our own darkness on others and pretend that it didn't flow out of our own potential for manifesting darkness. The life of every human being on earth depends on this! The life of our planet depends on this. The potential to blow up and destroy Earth is within our reach, and to have that happen, because of the fear that could keep us from facing the negativity and destructiveness within ourselves would be a great sadness. How wonderful it is to let love reach its arms around us all and tenderly whisper the secrets of beauty that lie waiting within us! We are all the sleeping beauty in the fairytale, and life is the prince that comes to awaken us with a kiss.

We all dream about things we would like to do. If the dreams grow out of our fear of losing, we become entangled in wanting to hold on to what we have. Our lives become more about having than about living. We want to own what we want. Those who continue to live creatively and keep moving, making the most of each moment, are able to go beyond the obsession of 'havingness.' What they do is developed through talent and ability, and what they need to develop through practice. If talent is nurtured and developed, the creative power will help to bring the flow to life so that manifesting and creating becomes a natural result. Beethoven said, *"I change many things, discard others, and try again and again until I am satisfied. Then, in my head, I begin to elaborate the work in its breadth, its narrowness, its height, its depth... I hear and see the image in front of me from every angle, as if it had been cast, and only the labor of writing it down remains."*

Those who care about us tell us what we should be wearing to be more attractive and what we should be eating to be healthier. Looking better and feeling better helps to draw out the attraction. Beauty around us helps to develop the soul, to keep it young, to develop the soul of a lover, to express love as a way of life. Anyone can feel it when they hear children giggling in the playground and the nightingale singing in the garden to the rose.

Yesterday morning, I went into the garden to pick a rose to put on my desk. The rose decided not to come into my studio, and like a jealous lover, shed her petals. How thoughtless of me not to have brought it in sooner! The rose bloomed to reveal its beauty, for that creative power that spreads the aroma also quite naturally spreads the beauty. That is creativity! That is the rose living its creative life! The existence of the rose reaches far beyond our perception of its gift. The rose has much to give us, while most of us are only aware of one dimension. We have to develop and become a part of the creative process that flowers into beauty to enhance life.

The rose is attractive and carries the seeds to place in the snare, to become the bait, to lure us into bewilderment, to soften us like spring, to activate the power of love, and to open the heart. It has the fragrance that charms us into submission, which is what draws and attracts us to admire it. We are automatically attracted by the mysterious perfume that awakens the senses. If you hold a rose, it goes to your nose, no matter who you are.

If we could surrender to the beauty and the joy it brings, we would be able to create in multi-dimensional ways like the rose, not only in our dreams, but also in a reality that manifests all around us. It will leave a trail of our flowering, for it is the nature of love to blossom us into beauty and into a new way of seeing.

Longing is what consistently helps to maintain our connection to our creativity. Every time we experience longing, the energy helps to activate the flow, and the flow synchronizes with the energy of creation itself. The thrill brings us to life, as in the act of loving, as the waves of feeling continue expressing creatively from the heart, and it discovers the joyful rhythm and the ecstasy to elevate our participation in the wonder of life.

There are times when my energy has more creative power than my physical body or technical ability can handle. In such a condition, I am constantly creating, and I don't have time to manifest and integrate it with my life. At other times, my creative process becomes something that grows from the impulse that everyone can see and use. Which is the dream and which is the reality does not matter to me. I only feel the multi-dimensional power that harbors the diversity within me.

Most people give up creating in early childhood as they try to please the people around them who stifle the spirit by focusing their vision toward making a living to have what they want. From a very early age, we develop children and we teach them to judge by shaping their behavior to please us. We impress upon them that they have to be good and follow the rules.

Children would naturally manifest their inner beauty if the rational mind were not activated so early, stealing their innocence and childhood before they truly become aware of the wonder and freedom of creative play. The real development takes place *before* the child goes to school. It is wherever the flow takes place naturally as it does in the backyard, on the playground, in the sandbox, in the fields and meadows, the rivers and streams, and the old swimming hole where we touch the beauty and freedom of sharing our joy. The presentation of overflowing creativity follows the wonder as the cup of the heart runs over and becomes all we see, feel and experience.

Sometimes I wonder, what is more joyful, a fantasized romance, or the one we are able to hold in our arms. When we have the ability to combine both, we experience the maximum joy. Our creative process in this case is the ability to combine fantasy with the physical reality. The physical act helps us to manifest the fantasy in some creative way.

For most people, the difference between dream and reality is immense. It can seem to be a great distance to cover. For a creative person this is not true. There is such a difference between the two that it can seem overwhelming and beyond our ability to bring them together, so we tend to give up one and become occupied with one or the other. The two need to become parallel, to work together to develop the strength of vision. We engage the dream and coax it into reality.

If we freely create without limitation in the beginning, once we behold creation at work, we can manifest it into form that serves ourselves and others without having compromised our creative ability. In her famed book, *The Fountainhead*, Russian born American novelist, Ayn Rand, develops a story around the theme of the integrity of the vision of the architect to create from his own truth. It is the theme for much of our creativity to insist on the light of the truth to give it artistic license to change the rules, to bend the reality, to fight for the freedom to create, and not to produce some generic pattern over and over to put everyone to sleep.

American architect, Frank Lloyd Wright approaches a piece of land out in the nowhere of wilderness in order to design a building several stories high. Something in Wright's mind is attracting him to create. He chooses a place free of boundaries. It may not even be what his client wanted. He has a vision, and he finds the place that will allow it to develop. Then comes the moment when people want the vision that he has developed in his life. Following the creative impulse of the heart produces a life-giving energy, and it attracts others to the aroma of love that emanates from a person who lives out of that beauty.

Sometimes an apprentice tells me he can't paint without something to look at, because he wants to reflect what he sees onto the canvas. He isn't able to paint from the abstract and the unseen. My instruction to him is to look at something that he wants to paint for as long as he needs to be able to perceive the image fully in his mind. He is then able to quite easily make the image that is inside him visible on canvas without looking at the object. The artwork is about the artist and his feelings, not the object that is painted.

The process of presenting something in order to develop technical ability is not meant to be separated from the creative act as a whole. It becomes tedious and exhausting to try to be perfect and only representational. We simply end up repeating something over and over. We develop anxiety and depression, and feel the weight of trying to carry the burden ourselves, not realizing that love is waiting to help us ascend through a greater and more mysterious power than we could imagine.

Many teachers have students copy something for the discipline of it, to develop mastery of line and perspective. This develops technique. To do an exact likeness teaches control instead of creativity. It can help us practice, but it doesn't make us creative. We learn to change the rhythm in the dance of creating, improvising in every moment. A painter could do anything, even spit on the canvas, turn it around, upside down, and develop something new out of it. He can use the simplest thing to change the energy, using his culture, his belief system, his shortcomings, and put them out there as a part of his creation. The power that develops creativity is the mystery that flows from the heart. Love is an eternal energy that continually creates through us in a new way as if it were the first time we have ever seen the world, the first time that we have ever felt the joy of bursting into a life that is expressing us!

When we experience the power of love in our creativity, we begin to develop a total confidence, a blessed assurance of the companionship of the beloved. Love becomes our guide and friend. We distance ourselves from fear of criticism and realize that other people's criticism really only reflects their own discomfort. They are projecting what they feel about themselves on what we are doing.

To master our creative power, we learn from the greatest creator, which is nature. It is constantly throwing out what it creates to create something new. Nature becomes our teacher, because in throwing something away, we have no interest in going back over something to make it perfect or to spend the rest of our life trying to be a watchdog for what we have hoarded away.

Our greatest freedom comes through love. It is the freedom that lifts us over the threshold and connects us with the creative flow of life. Only one egg develops among the billions of creatures that return to earth in a drop of sperm, just as millions of seeds in creation are scattered to the wind. It makes hanging on to what we create seem quite insignificant when we view it in that overall perspective. Nature doesn't copyright its beauty. It builds on it to keep creating!

As long as we are creating our own life, why not make it our masterpiece! This is the unique work that no one else will ever own. Let others express themselves through their connection with you! Let them tell you what they see in you, and when they do, you learn something about them, about who they are and about what matters to them. This is how creating our own life leads to others creating through us.

When our imagination and manifestation become as liberating and as free as nature, and we are no longer attached to anything that comes through us, then life becomes a creative flow. When we can do that with joy, we bring creativity into our whole existence, and it deeply affects how we live and who we become. Love takes us one step further, elevates our joy and expands it into a divine compassion for all creation desiring that every heart might find its fullness in the gift of life.

ABOUT THE AUTHOR

RASSOULI is known in the art world for his stunning and insightful artworks. He is an artist of life, one who lives and expresses whatever he does from his heart. He describes himself as an ogler and a libertine, as one who sees beneath the surface, one who is free to express what he sees and feels and imagines! Whoever you thought he was yesterday, you can be sure he will bring something fresh and new to today, and he will surely come up with something fun for tomorrow.

Rassouli has inspired, invited, and encouraged creativity around the world through a process he calls Fusionart, which activates the creative power of the heart, expressing the wonder and the sensual beauty of the soul. He speaks about creativity in person, in his retreats, through articles and books and talks to groups, on the radio, in videos, and in films, and nowhere does he do it more magically than through his paintings.

Rassouli throws rules to the wind and dives into the moment and savors it, and his excitement for the process affects and stimulates everyone around him to do the same! He paints with rags, with his hands, and uses his favorite brushes when he feels moved to enhance what is happening on the canvas. He usually begins with a canvas primed with black paint and brings the light of vision to it, developing a relationship with the emerging image as he progresses.

Rassouli is presently living in Southern California to paint beauty, create inventive and original architectural designs, write books and articles and offer retreats to develop creativity in people of all ages and abilities around the world. Rassouli is dedicated to this vision and greatly excited about the value of creativity in changing lives. He is always searching for new ways to express this and invite every heart to discover their own unique ways of sharing.

You can visit his websites below to find out more about the seminars and retreats he runs on creativity and other topics, as well as his artwork.

www.Rassouli.com
www.FreydoonRassouli.com
www.AvatarFineArts.com
www.NewDawnCollections.com
www.FusionartInternational.com

ALSO AVAILABLE FROM BLUE ANGEL PUBLISHING

Rumi Revealed
Selected Poems from the Divan of Shams
Direct Translations & Mystical Expressions by Rassouli

Rumi has been introduced to the western world primarily as a poet, but the scope of his creative power and the range of his vision shine far beyond the literary genre of poetry. Rumi was often in an exalted state when he shared the revelations of his poetic expression. Playing a sitar and singing and dancing his joy wherever he went, Rumi exhibited a tireless energy to proclaim the unlimited potential of the human being. Many centuries later, we are still mining truth from the work of this visionary mystic. Rumi has hidden the secrets of the universe in his metaphors and stories and offers a continuing invitation to be true to the expressions of the heart. One verse can open a vision to reveal the richness and beauty of a new life hidden within our dreams and imagination. In *Rumi Revealed*, mystic artist and author Rassouli, who was raised as a Sufi, reveals the deeper essence of Rumi through his direct translations and visionary interpretations of Rumi's ecstatic verses.

Paperback book, 260 pages.

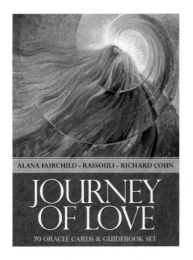

Journey of Love Oracle
by Alana Fairchild, Rassouli and Richard Cohn

Featuring 70 illuminating paintings by visionary artist Rassouli, the cards in *Journey of Love* are bursting with vibrant hues and stunning mystical depictions of feminine and natural beauty that help you connect deeply with the love that is at the very heart of everything in existence. Accompanied by exquisite poetic verses by Richard Cohn and profound messages of guidance by Alana Fairchild, these cards are designed to assist you to find your authentic path through the opportunities for growth presented to you in all aspects of life, especially in your relationships, not only with others, but in your sacred relationship with yourself.

70 cards and detailed 164-page guidebook, packaged in a hard-cover box set.

ALSO AVAILABLE FROM BLUE ANGEL PUBLISHING

Wild Kuan Yin Oracle
by Alana Fairchild - Artwork by Wang Yiguang

Within you beats a wild and compassionate heart, alive with fierce optimism. You have the courage to walk a path of transformation. You will not be tamed by convention. You are not afraid to be different, to take risks for what you love, and most of all, to keep hope in your heart. You are one of the wild ones. This deck is for you. *Wild Kuan Yin Oracle* will be your light in those moments when the darkness seems too much. When the loving peace of Spirit seems too far away from the troubles of the physical world, this oracle deck channels the energy of the Divine Mother to bring you comfort. She'll guide you through even the darkest trials into the blessing of new life. She'll open your heart and mind to untold possibilities and assist you to live your highest destiny with fearlessness and joy.

44 cards and 272-page guidebook set, packaged in a hard-cover box.

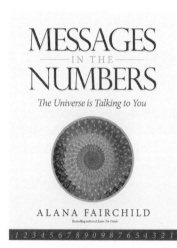

Messages in the Numbers
by Alana Fairchild

This book holds the key to decoding the secret messages in the numbers you notice around you – those repeating patterns on your phone, alarm, computer screen or the digital clock in your car, and even in significant dates, your house number or the number plates on the cars you drive past. The Universe wants to help you! And one of the ways it does that is by sending you messages through numbers. These are messages that the Universe wants to get through to you – to help you grow and live a happier, more connected and fulfilling life. Are you ready to hear them? It's easy! Let this super-practical guidebook help you interpret the messages in the numbers so you can receive the guidance that is meant for you. Features simple guided meditative processes and sacred geometry images to help you connect energetically with each number's vibration.

Paperback book, 232 pages.

ALSO AVAILABLE FROM BLUE ANGEL PUBLISHING

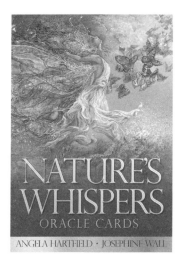

Nature's Whispers Oracle Cards
by Angela Hartfield - Illustrated by Josephine Wall

Nature is continually enticing us to spend time in embrace, through the calling of birds, the babbling brooks and streams, the fragrant smell of the flowers and the whispers of the trees as the wind blows through their branches. Through this vibrant deck, featuring the exquisite artwork of Josephine Wall, nature beckons you to experience a world of profound beauty and timeless wisdom. Re-ignite your connection to the great spirit of Mother Earth and tap into the profound peace, healing and guidance she offers us – if we only take a moment to listen.

50 cards and 72-page guidebook set, packaged in a hard-cover box.

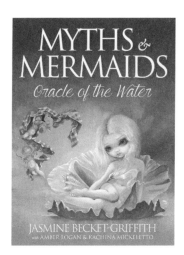

Myths & Mermaids: Oracle of the Water
by Jasmine Becket-Griffith
with Amber Logan & Kachina Mickeletto

The mystical element of water is both bringer of life and bearer of death, the herald of hope and the harbinger of destruction. It is in our nature to seek to understand it, to conquer it, and to sip its mysterious powers. Who better, then, to ask for guidance and inspiration than the spirits of water themselves, the Water Fae? Mermaids, sprites, nymphs, and more — their wisdom and insight have been collected within this oracle to help us comprehend and embrace the enigmatic dichotomy that is water. *Myths & Mermaids* features the artwork of world-renowned artist Jasmine Becket-Griffith, paired with a guidebook channelling the wisdom, advice, and poignant poetry of Jasmine's two sisters, Amber Logan and Kachina Mickeletto. Embrace the duality that is the element of water and prepare to plumb the depths of the unknown with guidance from the Water Fae!

44 cards and 120-page guidebook set, packaged in a hard-cover box.

For more information
on this or any
Blue Angel Publishing® release,
please visit our website at:

www.blueangelonline.com